Managing Perfo

...in brie.

C000027250

This book is dedicated to:
The memory of my mother and father
My wife Laura and my children Jenny, Susan and Peter

Managing
Performance
. . . in brief

Sultan Kermally

BUTTERWORTH
HEINEMANN

Butterworth-Heinemann
Linacre House, Jordan Hill, Oxford OX2 8DP
A division of Reed Educational and Professional Publishing Ltd

A member of the Reed Elsevier plc group

OXFORD   BOSTON   JOHANNESBURG
MELBOURNE   NEW DELHI   SINGAPORE

First published 1997

British Library Cataloguing in Publication Data
A catalogue record for this book is available from the British Library

ISBN 0 7506 3607 6

Composition by Scribe Design, Gillingham, Kent
Printed and bound in Great Britain by
Biddles Ltd, Guildford and King's Lynn

Contents

Acknowledgements

My very sincere thanks first of all go to Jacquie Shanahan of Butterworth-Heinemann for provoking me to write a book on 'Managing performance' covering the interests of all stakeholders. I could not resist the challenge.

This book was written with the help of the following individuals and organizations. My sincere thanks to all of them.

- Arthur D. Little, Cambridge, Massachusetts, USA
- Avis Management Services Ltd, UK
- American Management Association for allowing me to reprint from *Organizational Dynamics*
- Business Week, USA
- Dr Bruce Lloyd, Principal Lecturer in Strategy at South Bank University, London
- Business In the Environment, London
- BSI, London
- Council of Science and Technology Institute, London.
- Coopers & Lybrand, London, especially Victor Luck.
- Customer Service Management, London
- Digital Equipment Company, UK
- John Humble
- The Economist Intelligence Unit, London
- The Economist Conferences, London
- The Financial Times, London
- Fortune, USA.
- Global Finance Media, Inc.
- Harvard Business School Publishing. Copyright 'President and Fellows of Harvard College'; all rights reserved
- John Ainley, Group HR Director, W. H. Smith Group plc, London for information on 'Using feedback in the Performance Management Process'
- John Kelly, Managing Director, European Quality, England
- Kevin Dunkeld, Manager Personnel Services, Federal Express Europe Inc.
- Lesley Colyer, Vice President – Personnel, AVIS Management Services Ltd, England

Acknowledgements

- Mike Roberts, Manager, Customer satisfaction & quality, Sun Microsystems Computer Company, UK
- Mark Barthel, EMS Product Manager, BSI Training Services, London
- Management Centre Europe, Brussels
- Robert Gray, Manager–Purchasing, Nissan Motor Manufacturing (UK) Ltd.
- The Sunday Times, London
- Steve Crabb, editor, *Supply Management*, England
- Towers Perrin, London
- All the staff at Butterworth-Heinemann who are handling this project, especially Jacquie Shanahan for giving me this opportunity to increase my learning, Kathryn Grant for her faith in me, and Diane Scarlett and Sarah Leatherbarrow for their professional handling.

Finally, my affection and thanks go to my wife Laura for her enthusiasm in my work and for her support and to my children Peter, Susan and Jenny for their pride and encouragement.

Sultan Kermally
1997

Introduction

in brief

To go on a voyage of discovery you don't need new landscape, you need fresh eyes.
Unknown

Summary

This chapter provides brief information on:
■ Major drivers and influences affecting many organizations today
■ Categorization of these drivers and influences
■ The need for organizations to track their performance
■ The need for readers to remember that measurement is not management
■ The topics chosen for this book

Performance management is used as the organization's steering wheel, helping all parts of the organization to move together in the right direction. If the various departments' activities and operations are not aligned to what the organization has set out to achieve, it will be difficult to steer smoothly.

Fundamental questions many organizations are asking today are:

■ How can we translate our corporate strategy into action and reality?
■ How are departmental and individual objectives aligned to our corporate objectives?
■ How can we enhance shareholder value?

Managing Performance

- Do we need to balance the expectations and interests of all stakeholders or focus our attention on stockholders?
- Who are the stakeholders?
- What kind of measurement system should we use in an ever-changing business climate?
- What is wrong with our traditional financial measures which have served us so well for so long?
- How do we make measurements meaningful to all stake-holders?
- What drivers of business performance do we need to focus our attention on?
- If we are talking about 'customer focus' and 'values' and 'teaming', should we incorporate such concepts in our performance appraisal system?
- What drives high performance organizations?

These and other questions have become the focus of discussion and debate in the late 1990s.

Drivers of and influences on performance – the world has changed

The main drivers of organizational performance can be categorized into external drivers and influences and internal drivers and influences. **External** drivers consist of STEP factors, competition, customers and stockholders. **Internal** drivers consist of employees, top management, leadership, corporate culture, and the processes and products of the organization.

External drivers

1 STEP factors

These are the Sociological, Technological, Economic and Political (STEP) factors affecting organizations. Sociological factors include social values and attitudes, life styles, structure of household, demographic changes, attitude towards environmental issues, cultural differences, process of cultural assimilation and so on which impact upon factors

2

affecting demand for goods and services. Organizations have to respond to such demands in order to remain competitive.

Technological factors include the spread of the information infrastructure within organizations and within society. New technologies and skills are becoming increasingly diffused and organizations, big and small, are becoming high-tech.

In the computing and telecommunication areas, developments are taking place at breathtaking pace. More and more technologies are converging to make the 'global village' a reality.

From a business perspective, technological developments are enabling organizations to flatten their structures and pass decision making down the line in order to be more responsive to market needs. Technology is used to underpin corporate strategy.

Economic factors such as inflation, employment levels, government expenditures, trade balances, changing exchange rates, the development towards a single currency and so on affect business decisions. Options and futures markets serve businesses to cushion their exchange rate changes in order to minimize the impact on their investments.

Political factors such as the decision to privatize public sector organizations and deregulation have provided new sources of competition. Political dogmas are being discarded to accommodate the globalization process and the political climate is changing from conflict to collaboration. There are now numerous acquisitions, strategic partnerships and global supply chains established across international borders.

The world indeed has changed and the future is not what it used to be!

2 Competition

Competition is no longer confined to a few geographic blocs. Many businesses are competing in the international arena. Countries like India, Singapore, Korea, Taiwan, Chile and Argentina, to name but a few, are competing intensively with once economically powerful countries like America, the UK and Germany.

Managing Performance

Transnational and global deals are made to strengthen competitive positions and the economics of speed has become the essence of competition. The following are 10 observations as to what is happening in the competitive arena:

A Product life cycles are shortening.
B Product ranges are broadening.
C Product development processes are speeding up.
D Supply chains are shortening and are being developed globally.
E Organizations are achieving greater breakthroughs in time performance.
F Lead times are getting shorter.
G Customers have more choice and are becoming more demanding.
H Organizations are becoming more responsive to customer demands.
I   Customers want high quality and lower costs.
J Organizations have constantly to add value for their customers.

The profile of business is changing dramatically because of the pressures of competition.

3 Customers

Customers now have many choices and are becoming very discriminating. They make use of technology (the Internet) to scan availability of goods and services. They no longer tolerate production-centred organizations (and there are still many such organizations).

Organizations in turn try to focus their attention on customers and to produce products and introduce processes to increase their responsiveness to customer needs.

Apart from satisfying customers' needs, customer retention has gained important significance and the business world is now buzzing with phrases like 'relationship marketing', 'customer loyalty', etc.

Introduction

4 Stockholders

Stockholders have invested their capital in businesses and they rely on top management to be the custodian of their investment and to produce reasonable yields on their investments.

Financial analysts examine the financial performance of organizations and investors do take notice of such analysis. In recent years we have seen boardroom coups and the departure of numerous chief financial executives because their organizations have delivered poor financial performance or performance below budget expectations.

Internal factors

1 Leadership

The leadership's values and mission drive business performance. If the corporate values and strategy are communicated openly, honestly and clearly all the way down the organization, such an organization will see an improvement in its performance.

2 Employees

Employees are a group of direct stakeholders. Their motivation, competencies and aspirations will drive the business forward and impact upon its performance. Employees' objectives should be consistent with organizational objectives. Their performance depends on how they are managed and how their performance is measured.

3 Corporate culture

Corporate culture provides the context within which business decisions are made and implemented. If the culture is intolerant or intimidating or unfair then organizational performance will be affected unfavourably.

4 Product and processes

Organizations constantly have to keep their products and processes under review. Without such a review they will not be able to satisfy customers' needs.

External and internal factors drive performance. The question is, is the organization moving along the right track? There has been a marked increase in interest in performance measurement in recent years. This increase has gone hand in hand with a shift of emphasis towards non-financial and less aggregated measures that directly reflect and stimulate improvement in strategic operational performance. 'What you count, counts' or 'What gets measured gets done' may not be completely satisfactory.

Measurement is not management. To manage and sustain high performance requires credibility, conviction, commitment, and honest and open communication from the leadership. Also, what is important is that organizations manage the drivers of high performance and not the results. Management also involves putting in place appropriate systems of implementation and monitoring.

Performance measurement and management play key roles in translating business strategy into results. Results need to be assessed, monitored and reviewed continuously in order to sustain high performance and remain competitive in the marketplace.

About this book

This book addresses all the fundamental questions raised above. It starts with the **stakeholders' perspective** in managing performance. Management performance is about taking care of all stakeholders' interests and aspirations. It is also about putting internal and external focus on various drivers affecting business performance. The concept of the balanced scorecard is introduced in this context.

The way this is done depends on the **quality of leadership and its performance**. The performance of leaders and their values play key roles in motivation and in achieving desired results. Leaders have responsibility for developing an integrative vision for their organizations.

Introduction

The traditional measures of many organizations are financial. Various **financial measures** and ratios are formulated to measure the performance of return on assets, price/earnings ratio, stock turnover, working capital and the like. **Shareholders** as a group of stakeholders are interested in finding out how their investment is performing. The leadership has to consider how to enhance shareholder value. In this context new measurement concepts have been introduced to focus on value-based management.

Employees are among the key stakeholders and their motivation and expectations affect organizational performance. Their performance should be appraised appropriately and the objectives set for their performance should be consistent with corporate objectives.

Most organizations today strive to deliver service excellence. What matters today is not only what is produced but how it is delivered. The process of delivery incorporates customers' experience and empathy.

Measuring customer satisfaction, loyalty and **repeat business** has become major activities in many organizations like Avis, Sun Microsystems and Federal Express. Their experiences in this area are highlighted in this book.

Environmental considerations are now becoming major considerations affecting costs and thus impacting organizational performance. Such considerations improve business processes and promote innovation and creativity. What was once given peripheral consideration has become one of the key enablers of high performance. **Environmental management** is presented in this book as a key performance enhancer.

High performance does not take place in a vacuum. **Corporate culture** provides the internal context within which decisions are made. Bullying, discrimination, playing power games and stress have debilitating effects on organizational performance. A culture devoted to learning, innovation, empowerment and diversity will enable an organization to respond to the marketplace effectively.

Finally the book examines the measurement of **economic performance** and economic variables as they affect business performance. Micro-economic and macroeconomic variables relate to and affect business performance.

Covering various dimensions of measuring and managing performance, this book is presented in very simple language focusing on the interests and management of all stakeholders.

Selected reading

Drucker, P. (1995). *Managing in a Time of Great Change*. Butterworth-Heinemann.
Kermally, S. (1996). *Total Management Thinking*. Butterworth-Heinemann.

Performance management – time out

in brief

You can succeed in everything with a proper effort.
Theocritus

In our lives we are so occupied with doing what we are paid to do that we hardly have time to think. Thinking is a skill which enables us to evaluate our actions. Thinking time is an investment in self and as a consequence improves our personal performance.

One way of thinking about any issue or problem or topic is to raise a variety of questions in our minds and then set aside a time to focus on answers (take 'time out'). The answers we come up with constitute a fair reflection of our mindset on that particular issue or problem.

What follows is a series of questions on performance management. Read these questions and come up with your own answers. After that, continue reading this book and at the end come back to these questions and see if you have altered your views or your responses.

This is a structured way to fine-tune your mindset.

1. What do you understand by performance management?

Managing Performance

2. Do you differentiate between performance measurement and performance management?
3. What is the difference between performance measures and performance indicators?
4. How is the financial performance of an organization measured?
5. Are you aware of the latest developments in financial measures?
6. How is employee performance measured?
7. Are you aware of the latest developments in measuring employee performance?
8. What do you understand by 360-degree appraisal?
9. What aspects of employee performance should be measured?
10. What is the importance of the corporate mission and strategy in performance management?
11. Why is it important for departmental objectives to be consistent with corporate objectives?
12. Why is effective leadership important in achieving high performance?
13. What in your opinion is an appropriate leadership style in achieving high performance?
14. How do leaders measure their performance?
15. Should good leaders align their personal and professional aspirations with the aspirations of their followers?
16. How can one measure leadership?
17. Do personal values matter in good leadership?
18. What in your view are the characteristics of good leaders?
19. Are you aware of a debate on stakeholders vs. stockholders?
20. What is your view on this debate?
21. Who are the major stakeholders of an organization?
22. Do you consider such a debate to be of any value in understanding performance management?
23. How should a company balance the interests of all stakeholders?
24. Have you come across the concept of the balanced scorecard?
25. What areas does the scorecard measure?
26. What are the advantages of adopting a balanced scorecard?

10

Performance management – time out

27. Why is the customer service perspective important in performance management?
28. How do organizations measure customer satisfaction?
29. Do environmental issues enter into consideration in performance management?
30. How can environmental considerations enhance business performance?
31. Do you know of companies who have enhanced their business performance by considering environmental issues?
32. Have you heard of the existence of Business In the Community?
33. What is the role of corporate culture in managing performance?
34. What does corporate culture mean to you?
35. Why should organizational bullying, discrimination and stress at work affect business performance?
36. Do you agree that the value system within an organization is one of the most powerful drivers of business performance?
37. What is the link between customer satisfaction and employee satisfaction?
38. Are you aware of the mission of your organization?
39. Would you consider that all employees should be aware of the corporate mission?
40. Would you agree that managing performance requires consideration of customers, employees, suppliers, investors and the community at large?

YOU ARE NOW READY TO READ THIS BOOK.

In every chapter you are asked to take 'time out' (thinking time) to reflect on the issues raised.

Managing performance – for whose benefit?

in brief

It's easier to act ourselves into a new way of thinking than it is to think ourselves into a new way of acting.

Richard Pascale

Summary

■ All organizations measure their performance one way or another. Most of them rely on traditional financial measures.
■ How and what is measured reflects the corporate thinking and culture.
■ There are various dimensions of performance measurement – qualitative and quantitative and financial and non-financial.
■ There have not been many 'gurus' on performance measurement and management with the exception of Professor Robert Kaplan and Dr David Norton.
■ The current debate on performance management is presented as **Stakeholders' vs. Stockholders'** interests.

Stakeholders include management, employees, customers, suppliers, shareholders and the community at large. Stockholders generally reflect the interests of shareholders – those who have invested capital in the company.

■ Many organizations now are making efforts to integrate or align the organization's performance to employees' performance by formulating incentive and profit share schemes.

■ In the early 1990s Robert S. Kaplan, Professor at Harvard Business School, and Dr David P. Norton, the founder and President of Renaissance Solutions, introduced the balanced scorecard concept and approach to measuring an organization's performance. In 1996 they extended the scorecard to serve as a strategic management system.

■ The balanced scorecard is about alignment of corporate values with operational objectives, customer satisfaction, shareholder value and expectations, and individual employees' objectives, competencies and aspirations.

■ The balanced scorecard should be used with caution.

Dimensions of measurement

Managing organizational performance plays a very important part in translating corporate strategy into results. In the past, the focus of attention has been on measuring financial performance; in the 1970s and 1980s an additional focus was put on employees' performance, known as staff appraisals.

Quantitative and qualitative performance

There are different ways of measuring performance (Figure 1.1). Some organizations measure financial results, the performance of their employees, the quality of service provided to their customers, employees' attitude and morale, absenteeism, the quality of processes and products, innovation and creativity and so on. All these measures can be divided into qualitative and quantitative categories.

Managing Performance

Family of measures
(Some examples)

Qualitative	Quantitative
• Staff morale	• Turnover of staff
• Management style	• Absenteeism rate
• Bullying	• Return on capital
• Discrimination	• Profit per person
• Standard of safety	• Accidents per project

Financial	Non-financial
• Return on investment	• Hospital beds waiting list
• Liquidity ratios	• Number of female employees
• Gross margin	• Customers' complaints
• Gearing	• Defect rate
• Cost per project	• Product–lead time

Quantitative measures such as financial ratios, waiting lists for hospital beds, staff turnover, number of customers' complaints etc. are easy to measure and manage. Remember, 'What gets measured gets done'. As Ralph Kilmann in his book *Beyond the Quick Fix* puts it, "In most cases, measures are considered objective when hard numbers based on a well-formulated system of counting are available. Objectivity is thus more apparent when discrete quantities of value added are available, such as number of units produced, dollars of sales generated, dollars of costs saved, and numbers of clients generated."

Qualitative measures, such as motivation, morale, style of leadership and customers' perception, are difficult to measure and the way they are managed depends on the corporate agenda. If an organization is very serious in managing this aspect they will go out of their way to try to get measurement right. If, however, they simply treat such factors as 'soft' issues or if they introduce measurement as a window-dressing exercise, then its management becomes ineffective.

In the report 'The New Look of Corporate Performance Measurement' published by the Economist Intelligence Unit in association with KPMG in 1994, the message put forward was that the 1990s were going to be the decade with a difference. More than 70 per cent of respondents in the survey stated that they were dissatisfied with their company's performance measurement system.

The report indicated that change was afoot in measuring corporate performance. The main forces driving change are:

Managing performance – for whose benefit?

- the accelerated pace of business in the 1990s,
- empowering employees to respond to competitive pressures and market needs,
- deregulation and the opening up of new markets,
- competition from the Far East (the Asian tigers and potential tigers).

The new thinking demands that performance management should support corporate strategy formulation and monitor value drivers, i.e. those elements that really make the business profitable. How performance is measured and managed reflects corporate thinking. As one consultant has put it, "If companies are going to talk 'teamwork', 'values', and 'customer focus' then they need to start incorporating these concepts into their performance appraisal system."

TIME OUT

How does your organization measure performance?

_____

_____

_____

Categorize your organization's performance measures into quantitative and qualitative measures.

Quantitative: _____

_____

Qualitative: _____

_____

Gurus on performance management

This subject, like motivation, leadership, customer service, empowerment and the learning organization, has attracted many gurus. There are not many gurus in the field of performance management except Robert Kaplan and David Norton who put forward the concept of the balanced scorecard in 1992.

However, this does not mean that gurus like Tom Peters and Peter Drucker have nothing to say on the subject. Tom Peters, for example, has this to say on performance evaluation:

> Like the cost-accounting systems ... these systems started for useful reasons which (1) have become increasingly bureaucratic, run by 'experts' (often personnel departments in this case) ... and (2) are frighteningly out of touch with today's and tomorrow's needs. They are stability-inducing systems at odds with a world where flexibility is the chief survival requirement.
>
> Tom Peters: *Thriving on Chaos*

Most of the comments made on performance are focused on employee performance. Peter Drucker has this to say on employee satisfaction and performance:

> What motivation is needed to obtain peak performance from the worker? The answer that is usually given today in American industry is 'employee satisfaction'. But this is an almost meaningless concept. Even if it meant something 'employee satisfaction' would still not be sufficient motivation to fulfil the needs of the enterprise.
>
> A man may be satisfied with his job because he really finds fulfilment in it. He may also be satisfied because the job permits him to 'get by'. A man may be dissatisfied because he is genuinely discontented. But he may also be dissatisfied because he wants to do a better job, wants to improve his own work and that of his group, wants to do bigger and better things. And this dissatisfaction is the most valuable attitude any company can possess in its employees, and the most real expression of pride in job and work, and of responsibility. Yet we have no way of telling satisfaction that is fulfilment from satisfaction that

is just apathy, dissatisfaction that is discontent from dissatisfaction that is desire to do a better job.

Peter Drucker: *The Practice of Management*

A plethora of books have been written on performance appraisals and financial performance over the years. Increasingly the focus of attention is being put on new ways of measuring financial performance and new methods of appraising employees' performance (e.g. the 360-degree appraisal system).

Current debate on managing performance

The current debate on managing performance is characterized by various schools of thought.

School of thought 'A' – Shareholders' perspective

Some writers argue that the Board of Directors and top management are there to formulate strategy that accommodates the expectations of shareholders. Capital is necessary to create the process of value creation and it is shareholders who provide that capital and bear risks. Analysts monitor business performance and indirectly communicate their assessment to shareholders.

Shareholders are keen to know how their investments are performing. They are interested in key financial indicators and dividends. If shareholders' expectations are not managed then they will sell their shares and all the stakeholders within the business will be unfavourably affected.

In *The Sunday Times* of 2 February 1997 it was reported that as far as Sainsbury, the supermarket group, was concerned, the patience of shareholders was wearing thin after five years of decline. In January 1997 Sainsbury announced its third profit warning in four years and immediately the share price dropped and at one stage almost one billion pounds were cut from the company's market value. Shareholders are gunning for David Sainsbury, the chairman of the company.

Managing Performance

"Shareholder value is about the only game in town", say some analysts. Companies merge, de-merge and diversify, and chairmen and chief executives are hired and fired in order to enhance shareholder value. Some downsize their operations in order to increase return on equity.

Most chairmen and chief executive officers care very much what analysts write about their business. They are also looking for different ways to create shareholder value.

Recently some consultants have put forward new techniques of measuring corporate performance. These techniques are known as Market Value Added (MVA) and Economic Value Added (EVA). MVA measurement shows the total profit (excluding dividends) made over the years for the shareholders. EVA measures the difference between the return on capital and its cost. The difference is the value created by the company for its shareholders.

School of thought 'B' – Employees' perspective

According to this school, the most important stakeholders are the employees of the organization. They give the best part of their lives to organizations and at the end of the day, however brilliant the corporate strategy, it is employees who make things happen.

In my book *Total Management Thinking* I have argued that the success of any organization depends on satisfying and retaining its customers. This means that organizations have to deliver service excellence.

But service is delivered by employees and not systems. Now employees will only deliver service excellence if they feel good about their organizations. Employees should feel 'I am OK, you are OK' towards their jobs and their organizations.

Employees also view their situation from three perspectives. They are: What I like to do, What I have to do, and What I am able to do.

Trust is also another major driving force in injecting the 'I'm OK' feeling. It has become the most important factor in achieving effective empowerment. Trust also has become one of the key attributes of a successful leader in the 1990s. Trust comes about when there is a series of positive encounters. Such positive encounters are characterized by allowing people to make mistakes, empowering your staff to make decisions, open communication and fair treatment.

Sultan Kermally: *Total Management Thinking*

Apart from financial performance it is very important to measure employees' performance. Employees' performance measurement should be consistent with corporate objectives. If employees make things happen in organizations then there has to be a congruence between corporate objectives and employees' performance objectives.

Considering employees as the main stakeholders of an organization and treating them as an appreciating asset and investing in them will enhance organizational performance which in turn will meet the expectations of the shareholders of organizations and keep analysts happy. Focusing attention on employees is, therefore, not an ideological issue but a business issue. To use a cliché, '**People mean Profit**'.

Integrating financial performance and people performance

Many organizations in the past few years have introduced incentive and profit share schemes based on financial performance. Here is an example of how a small company rewards its employees.

The company sets the corporate budget which then drives the budgets of all divisions and departments. The two guiding factors are increase in revenue (say 10 per cent) and increase in contributions (say 20 per cent). All divisions then prepare their budgets accordingly. This is a top-down budget process.

The incentive scheme is based on performance at corporate level and performance at divisional level. If the organization as a whole achieves its budget but one or more divisions exceed their budget targets then employees in those divisions receive a bonus based on their pay. How much bonus is paid is determined at the time of preparing the budget.

If the organization exceeds its budget and some of the divisions also exceed their budgets, the employees in those divisions receive two sets of bonuses, one based on corporate success and the other on their divisions' success.

Managing Performance

If a division has not achieved its budget but the organization has exceeded its budget target then employees get one bonus based on corporate success.

We will not go into the pros and cons of such an incentive system. The example is given to show how organizations manage shareholders' expectations by linking employees' performance to corporate financial targets.

The new method of measuring corporate performance, the Economic Value Added (EVA) method, is also being used to link employee performance with employee compensation. This method is explained in Chapter 2. In an article in *Fortune*, 9 September 1996, the chief executive officer of Eli Lilly, Mr Randall Tobias, explained how his company has used EVA to link compensation with employees' performance. They first set EVA targets based on competitive factors. Each year they have to beat this target and each year the bar is raised. If the targets are met or exceeded then executives are paid a bonus. At present the incentive plan is applied to senior executives only. Gradually it will apply to all employees.

In the *Financial Times* of 23 October 1996, Wolfgang Munchau says that German companies are questioning the automatic dominance of shareholders. It was reported that Volkswagen, the carmaker, has emerged as one of the most outspoken sceptics of 'shareholder value', saying that 'workholder value' should carry equal weight.

The report says that overall there is a great deal of scepticism in German boardrooms about pure shareholder value.

For whose benefit should an organization undertake performance measurement?

_____

_____

Why?

_____

_____

For whose benefit does your organization undertake performance measurement?

_____

_____

TIME OUT

Shareholders vs. stakeholders – more debate

In the past companies have always been managed and performance measured on behalf of the owners. When the 'managerial revolution' came about, divorcing ownership from control, managers were appointed to run the business on behalf of the owners. When businesses became public companies the shareholders became the owners and the focus of attention shifted from owners/entrepreneurs to shareholders.

Today some writers argue that the primary focus of business management should be to enhance shareholder value. Performance measurement systems should be consistent with promoting shareholders' interests and managing their expectations.

There are other stakeholders and they play an important part but, apart from shareholders, all other groups should receive secondary attention.

Other writers argue that managers should pay attention to the expectations of not only shareholders but also employees of the company, their customers, their suppliers and the community within which they operate.

In evidence to a Stock Exchange-backed inquiry into corporate governance headed by Sir Ronnie Hempel, ICI chairman, the Centre for Tomorrow's Company says that chief executives and their boards appear to believe that it is their legal duty to concentrate attention only on pleasing current shareholders.

The Centre, established by the Royal Society for Arts, argues that it is the fiduciary duty of the directors to give due weight to all stakeholders.

In the Royal Society of Arts report, 'Tomorrow's Company' (1995), one chief executive maintained: "Increasingly business people are recognizing that their prosperity is directly linked to the prosperity of the whole community. The community is the source of their customers, employees, their suppliers and, with widespread share ownership, their shareholders."

John Neil, group chief executive of Unipart, believes that the success of any business depends on various stakeholders, in particular employees and suppliers. If one can

Managing Performance

manage employees' and suppliers' expectations and work as partners then businesses will be able to compete effectively by providing customers with what they want.

According to Ralph Kilmann, author of *Beyond Quick Fix*, "performance is viewed in many different ways, depending on which stakeholders are being considered. For example, stockholders emphasize return on investment, consumers emphasize quality and reliability of products, and the community emphasizes more jobs and clean air. Organizational success is creating and maintaining high performance and morale for all or most stakeholders over an extended period of time."

According to Edward A. Brennan, Chairman of Sears Roebuck, USA, in September 1992: "Corporate responsibility continues to mean many things to us. It is the fair and equitable treatment of all our stakeholders including associates, shareholders, customers and suppliers. It is our sense of concern for the well-being of the public at large and for our environment. And it is the time and money that we contribute toward the communities where we do business." (Source: Ray Wild, *How To Manage*)

According to Johnson and Johnson's values: "We believe our first responsibility is to doctors, nurses and patients, to mothers and fathers and all others who use our products and services .. We are responsible to our employees, the men and women who work with us throughout the world. Everyone must be considered as an individual ... We are responsible to the communities in which we live and work and to the world community as well ... Our final responsibility is to our stockholders ... "

This debate will continue for a few years to come. There will be managing directors and their boards who will come under pressure from business analysts and focus their attention on shareholders; there will also be companies who genuinely believe that other groups such as employees, customers and suppliers have an important stakeholding in the business and that managing their expectations will contribute to enhanced performance and business success.

From an ideological to a pragmatic perspective

In an article which appeared in the *Financial Times* on Monday, 10 February 1997, entitled 'Value in Human Resources', the authors Linda Bilmes, Konrad Wetzker and Pascal Xhonneux reveal the strong link between companies' investment in workers and stock market performance.

They undertook research in 10 industrial sectors covering more than a hundred German companies over the period 1987 to 1994. They considered various aspects of human resource management such as training expenditure per employee, number of layoffs relative to industry average, general human resource policies, flexible work hours, teaming, acquisition of skills and profit-sharing, and they concluded that companies which had employee focus produced a greater 'total shareholder return' (the sum of share price increases and dividends over a given period) than their competitors. Among their various conclusions they state that investors would do well to think about employee-focus when they make investment decisions.

We need more research to establish the link between enhanced performance and a stakeholder-focus strategy. We need to move away from an ideological mindset to a pragmatic approach in assessing business performance.

Path to business excellence and stakeholders' interests

In order to promote business excellence and adopt total quality throughout organizations, awards have been introduced to recognize quality achievements. In America there is the Malcolm Baldrige Award which was introduced in 1987.

To win the Baldrige Award companies have to submit an application describing their practices and performance in seven required areas. These are:

■ Leadership
■ Information and analysis

Managing Performance

- Strategic planning
- Human resource development and management
- Process management
- Quality results
- Customer focus and satisfaction

Leadership: In this category judges look for day-to-day commitment from senior executives. Personal involvement of senior staff and the company's quality values and public responsibility are evaluated.

Information and analysis: Judges examine the scope and management of quality data and information; how they are used to bring about continuous improvement.

Strategic quality planning: Examiners look for two or three goals set by companies and examine how well the companies have met them. The strategic quality plan should provide a blueprint for continuous improvements.

Human resource development and management: How are the employees managed and what steps are companies taking to develop their competencies? Are employees empowered to make decisions in order to facilitate quality improvements? What methods are the company using to measure employee performance?

Management of process quality: Judges seek to determine how well companies understand what processes constitute critical processes. Other aspects judges look at in this category are the design and introduction of quality products and services; process quality control; quality assessment process; support service quality and supplier quality.

Quality results: Companies have to achieve continuous improvement in critical operational areas. Companies have to show high levels of performance relative to their competitors or that the company has benchmarked its operations against the best firm.

Customer focus and satisfaction: This is the most heavily weighted category. Examiners review a number of sources of information, including customer surveys, sales calls, customer focus groups and so on. Examiners look for how customers' requirements are met; customer relationship management; complaint resolution for quality improvement; customer satisfaction results and customer satisfaction comparison, which involves comparison with competitors.

Managing performance – for whose benefit?

The above categories are highlighted to guide companies to produce quality products and deliver quality service. In doing so they address the expectations of shareholders, customers and employees.

The award that takes on board the needs of key stakeholders is the European Quality Award which was developed by the European Foundation for Quality Management in 1992.

The model (shown in Figure 1.2) incorporates 'enablers' and 'results'. 'Enablers' are leadership, people management, policy and strategy, resources and processes, and 'results' are people satisfaction, customer satisfaction, impact on society and business results. We will highlight categories that have a direct impact on various stakeholders incorporated in the model. They are leaders, employees, customers, shareholders and society.

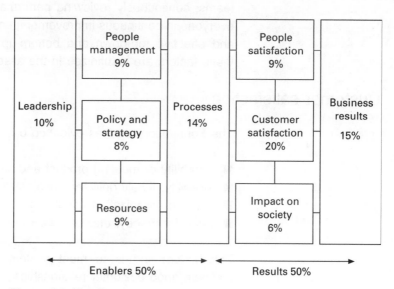

Figure 1.2 The European model

Leadership

Leadership is key to any business or organizational performance. As far as assessing total quality is concerned, visible involvement of the leadership becomes an important factor. Among many factors, the Foundation looks at:

Managing Performance

- the way the leadership communicates corporate values and culture,
- timely recognition and appreciation of the efforts and successes of individuals and teams,
- involvement with suppliers and customers, and
- active promotion of total quality outside the company.

Within this category alone, the interests of suppliers, customers and employees are taken on board.

People management

How the company releases the full potential of its people to improve the business continuously is examined. Evidence is required of how human resources are planned and improved; the skills and capabilities of the people and their development; agreements of targets by individuals and teams; continuously reviewing performance; involvement of everyone in continuous improvement; empowering of people and effective top-down and bottom-up communication; all these factors are scrutinized in the assessment process.

Customer satisfaction

The Foundation requires evidence on:

- capability of meeting product and service specifications,
- reliability, timely delivery, customer care,
- how the organization handles complaints,
- value for money, etc.

The bottom line is to meet customer requirements and maintain good customer relationships.

People satisfaction

Employees have aspirations and needs. This category focuses on the organization's efforts to meet those aspirations and needs in relation to providing a good working environment, job security, and career development reward and recognition.

Impact on society

This is a broad category covering the efforts the organization is making in satisfying the needs and expectations of the community at large. This involves support for charity, involvement in education and training, environment, impact on local employment etc.

Business results

This category examines the way the organization is going about achieving its business objectives. The focus is on financial and non-financial measures of the organization's success.

Shareholder value – What's in a name?

I think the debate about shareholder value or workholder value or stakeholder value is based on what these terms mean and how they are defined. In my view all companies want to enhance their shareholder value. This does not mean that they focus their attention on financial measures and pander to the interests of shareholders alone.

Shareholders hold shares in the hope that the company will perform well and achieve good returns for them. Some of them buy and sell shares in order to make a quick profit on their investment. There is nothing wrong in this practice. What is important, however, is that for the sake of all concerned the company must perform well financially. To do so it needs good leadership, capable and committed employees, suppliers who can be partners, and satisfied customers. In achieving business success the value of the shares will increase and thereby enhance shareholder value. The term shareholder value embraces the efforts, interests and expectations of all those involved in an enhanced business performance.

Arrival of the balanced scorecard

Professor Robert S. Kaplan of Harvard Business School and Dr David P. Norton, President of Renaissance Strategy Group, formulated a new measurement system that provided executives with a comprehensive framework to translate a company's strategic objectives into a meaningful set of performance measurements. This new system was the balanced scorecard approach. Their article 'The Balanced Scorecard – Measures that Drive Performance' was published in *Harvard Business Review*, January–February 1992.

The balanced scorecard is viewed from four perspectives:

- Financial
- Customers
- Internal processes
- Growth and learning

These four perspectives focus attention on internal and external influences affecting business performance. Many companies use the same systems of performance measurement, focusing on financial and cost performance, that they have used for several decades. Due to the dramatic change in the profile of business over the past decade, these measures have become outdated if organizations want to rely on reliable and effective performance measures. It is argued that the balanced scorecard provides that focus and enables the organization to measure true performance.

A scorecard keeps score of your activities and operations in relation to corporate strategy. It is an effective tool for highlighting and reinforcing corporate strategy.

The technique emerged from KPMG-funded research in the USA and it was initially concerned with the evaluation of investment in IT. It is now widely used as a framework for the whole business.

Focus on four perspectives

Financial perspective

ROCE	Cashflow	Shareholder value
Operating expenses	Project profitability	Liquidity
Gearing ratio	Sales growth	Growth

Customer perspective

New products	Customer partnership	Customer ranking
Customer satisfaction index	Market share	Superior lead-time
Low defect levels	On-time delivery	Responsiveness

Process perspective

Cycle time	High yields	Time to market
Quality	Safety	Project performance

Growth and learning perspective

Revenue growth	Revenue per employee	Technology
Innovation	New product development	Employees' morale

The type of scorecard approach used will depend on the nature of the organization and the business. According to Michael Morrow of KPMG the balanced scorecard is now widely used as a framework for the whole business. The first significant application in Europe was by Aer Lingus and the largest to date is NatWest. The balanced scorecard aims to provide performance measures at strategic level, business unit level, process level and individual level.

At the conference on European HR Management organized by the Economist Conferences in February 1997, one of the speakers, Mr François Escher, Director of Organizational Learning and Development at **AT&T International**, explained that achievement of AT&T's mission and objectives means success in:

- **Strategy**: How do we create our future business?
- **Market**: How do we delight our customers?
- **Finance**: How do we look to our shareholders?
- **Operations**: How do our business processes add value?
- **Learning**: How do we sustain innovation?

These five perspectives are measured to monitor business success.

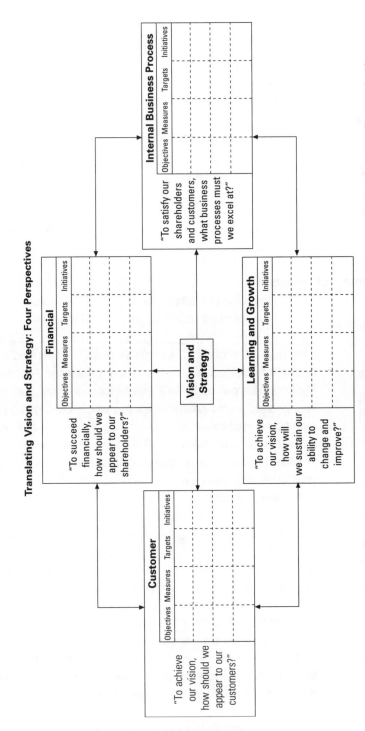

Figure 1.3 An example of a balanced scorecard. Translating vision and strategy: four perspectives. 1996; © 1996 by the President and Fellows of Harvard College; all rights reserved

Managing performance – for whose benefit?

At **Co-operative Bank**, according to Mr Ken Lewis, Executive Director, Group Resources, who spoke at the conference on 'Performance Management' organized by the Economist Conferences in February 1997, "We have taken the Bank's vision, aspiration and transformation goals and mapped them into the scorecard framework ... The scorecard is a key practical methodology through which we will deliver our plan consistently across the organization."

They track the following performance measures under various perspectives:

■ Financial perspective: Profit before tax, return on capital employed, bad debt ratio, revenue from new products, etc.
■ Internal businesses processes: Cost/income ratio, capacity potential, supplier satisfaction survey, value of products cross-sold, revenue from alliances, etc.
■ Customer perspective: Customer satisfaction index, market recognition index, ethical audit, number of initiatives targeted on profitable segments, number of community measures, etc.
■ Organization and learning perspective: Attrition rate, internal attitude survey, Investor in People certification, training days per member of staff per year, etc.

At **W. H. Smith Group** plc, John Ainley, Group Human Resource Director, says 'In one of our businesses we have been championing the balanced scorecard. This approach contends that the traditional financial measures tell but a part of the story. If it is only through complete customer satisfaction and loyalty that long-term superior results will occur then we should have customer satisfaction as a measure on our scorecard, and if staff satisfaction impacts on customer satisfaction, then that should also be on the scorecard. If our core competencies are going to develop our business then the effectiveness of our managers against the competencies ought to be measured and discussed at board level.'

S. G. Warburg track financial, internal processes, people and client perspectives and put a focus on vision. **Eurotunnel** track financial, process, learning and growth but put a focus on the safety perspective.

Implementation of a balanced scorecard starts from the top. The centrepiece of a balanced scorecard is the corpo-

Managing Performance

rate mission and strategy. The scorecard translates the mission and corporate strategy throughout the organization. **The essence of the scorecard is to capture corporate strategy in measurement**. It enables organizations to track financial measures while simultaneously monitoring progress in intangible areas of business which have become important in today's business climate (See Fig. 1.3).

TIME OUT

Design a balanced scorecard for your organization or department or section or team.

1. What is your corporate mission and strategy?

    _____

    _____

    _____

2. What would you incorporate under 'Financial Perspective'? (If we succeed how will we look to our shareholders?)

    _____

    _____

    _____

3. What would you incorporate under 'Internal Business Processes'? (What processes must we excel at?)

    _____

    _____

    _____

4. What would you incorporate under 'Innovation and Growth Perspective'? (How must our organization grow and learn?)

    _____

    _____

    _____

5. What would you incorporate under 'Customer Perspective'? (How must we look to our customers?)

    _____

    _____

    _____

New approach to balanced scorecard

Writing in *Harvard Business Review* (January–February 1996), Kaplan and Norton extended the use of the balanced scorecard. They presented the balanced scorecard as a new strategic management system. They write: "Managers using the balanced scorecard do not have to rely on short-term financial measures as the sole indicators of the company's performance. The scorecard lets them introduce four new management processes that, separately and in combination, contribute to linking long-term strategic objectives with short-term actions." Figure1.4 highlights these processes.

The first process, '**translating the vision**', enables an organization to express its vision and strategy as an integrated set of objectives and measures.

The second process, '**communicating and linking**', enables an organization to link corporate objectives with

Managing Strategy: four processes

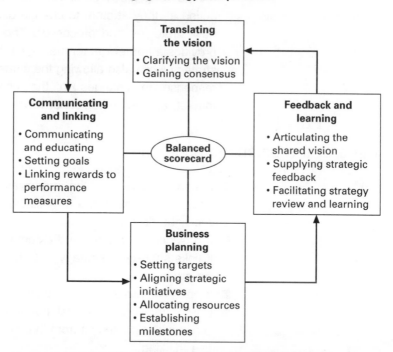

Figure 1.4 Managing strategy: four processes. Source: Using the balanced scorecard as a strategic management system. *Harvard Business Review*, January–February 1996. © 1996 by the President and Fellows of Harvard College; all rights reserved

Managing Performance

departmental and individual objectives, thus introducing consistency of objectives throughout the organization.

The third process, '**business planning**', brings business and financial planning into alignment.

The fourth process, '**feedback and learning**', develops organizational capacity for learning.

The balanced scorecard, therefore, according to Kaplan and Norton, can be used to develop a new strategic management system. They conclude:

> More recently, we have seen companies expand their use of the balanced scorecard, employing it as the foundation of an integrated and iterative strategic management system. Companies are using the scorecard to clarify and update strategy, communicate strategy throughout the company, align unit and individual goals with the strategy, link strategic objectives to long-term targets and actual budgets, identify and align strategic initiatives, and conduct periodic performance reviews to learn about and improve strategy.
>
> Without a balanced scorecard, most organizations are unable to achieve a similar consistency of vision and action as they attempt to change direction and introduce new strategies and processes. The balanced scorecard provides a framework for managing the implementation of strategy while also allowing the strategy itself to evolve in response to changes in the company's competitive market, and technological environments.

Uses of the balanced scorecard

- It can be used as the organization's steering wheel, helping all parts of the organization to move together in the right direction.
- It provides an internal and external focus.
- It links short-term strategy with the long-term strategy of an organization.
- It operationalizes the main drivers of business success.
- Unlike traditional financial performance, it changes an organization's mindset from 'has-been thinking' to proactive thinking.
- It encourages effective communication throughout the organization.
- It links corporate objectives with individual objectives.

- It co-ordinates all aspects of business.
- It enables the formulation of various scorecards through-out the organization.
- It focuses organizations' efforts in clearly defining their corporate objectives and translating them into action.
- It keeps measurement throughout the organization consistent and alive. 'What gets measured gets done.'
- It consolidates and reinforces corporate culture. 'The way we do business in our organization.'
- It is a tool for managing growth.

- The organization has to be culturally ready to use the balanced scorecard.

- The balanced scorecard focuses on what to achieve but not how to achieve desired results.
- Like a cricket scorecard it tells what happened and why it happened but not what produces a good score.
- It is a top-down approach.
- Measurement is not management.

Conclusion

Business should be managed and measured on a win-win basis. There should be high concern for investors (stock-holders) as well as all other stakeholders (Figure 1.5).

Figure 1.5 Balancing performance measurement

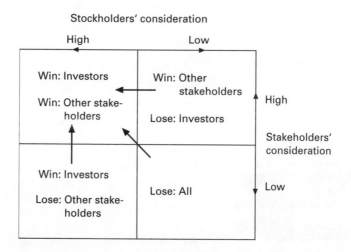

Selected reading

Boyett, J. H. and Henry, C. P. (1996). *Maximum Performance Management*. Capstone.

Kaplan, R. S. and Norton, D. P. (1992). The Balanced Scorecard – Measures that Drive Performance. *Harvard Business Review*, January–February.

Kaplan, R. S. and Norton, D. P. (1996). Using the Balanced Scorecard as a Strategic Management System. *Harvard Business Review*, January–February.

Kaplan, R. S. and Norton, D. P. (1996). *The Balanced Scorecard*. Harvard Business School Press.

Kermally, S. (1996). *Total Management Thinking – Ideas that are Transforming Management*. Butterworth-Heinemann.

Linge, J. H. and Schiemann, W. A. (1996). From Balanced Scorecard to Strategic Gauges: Is Measurement Worth It? *Management Review*, March.

Milan M. (1996). Bringing Performance Management Out of the Stone Age. *Management Review*, February.

Wild, R. (1994). *How To Manage*. Butterworth-Heinemann.

Effective leadership

in brief

Be the change you want to see in the world.
Mahatma Gandhi

Summary

■ For a number of years now management theorists have been trying to determine how leaders are able to produce a higher level of performance among their followers.

■ Since the beginning of the century various theories have been put forward relating to management and leadership styles. Among these theories were traits theories, behavioural theories, contingency theories and type theories.

■ Associated with various theories are managerial and leadership styles. Should leaders adopt an authoritarian or participative or democratic style in order to enhance organizational performance? Should leaders change their style depending on the circumstances they are facing or should they pay attention to the expectations, experience and competencies of their followers?

■ While debates on leadership styles and effectiveness prevail, the 1990s emerged as a period of dramatic change in the global market and competition. Competition emerged from every corner of the world. The Asian tigers emerged and shook many well-established corporations.

Managing Performance

■ In response to competition many organizations de-layered, restructured and re-engineered themselves and empowered their employees to respond to market and customer needs.

■ All the debates about the styles of leadership in my view have assumed less significance in the turbulent period we live in. Modern leaders have to establish 'rapport' with their employees and put emphasis on communicating values, and creating trust, credibility and integrity.

■ In the new millennium only those leaders who have integrity, values and credibility and who are trustworthy will be successful and will be able to enhance their organizational performance.

Performance comes through people. How you lead your people, therefore, becomes a very important factor in bringing about desired performance. The interest in studying leadership and leadership styles has practical significance. Various theories have been presented throughout this century and the search for the 'enlightened', 'transformational', 'servant-leader' and caring leader goes on.

Pioneers and theories

1900–70

For a number of years now management theorists have been asking questions on leadership: What makes a person a successful leader? Is a leader born or can a person be trained to become an effective leader? What is the best leadership style to achieve desired results?

Leadership is a process of influencing individuals and guiding others towards the desired goals. Leaders, therefore, have to be able to influence and provide necessary guidance to their followers. In order to perform their functions effectively leaders need to have power. Without power they will not be able to influence or exercise control or authority. The emphasis has always been on possession of power as the key element in the exercise of leadership. The sources of power, according to some theorists, are reward (granting of privilege or position), coercion (an individual's ability to coerce or force), legitimacy (official position) and referent (delegated or transferred power).

Effective leadership

According to James M. Burns, leadership is "one of the most observed and the least understood phenomenon on earth". Over the years various theories have been put forward by management writers. Most of these come from America. These theories have been categorized into:

- Trait theories
- Behavioural theories
- Contingency theories
- Type theories

Trait theories

Some theorists believed that leaders are born. Great leaders had inherent traits such as high intelligence, understanding of people, self-confidence and charisma. According to this school of thought leadership was a cluster of outstanding qualities within the leader.

Trait theories lost their popularity partly because it was difficult to measure or define them and partly because it was difficult to answer questions like 'what is the optimal combination of traits necessary for a successful leader?'

Management pioneers like Frederick W. Taylor and Henri Fayol believed in the trait approach. Because of various disagreements among scholars the search for other explanations of leadership began.

Behavioural theories

According to the behavioural school of thought leadership is the function of the behaviour of the individual.

Leadership behaviour exists on a continuum ranging from authoritarian behaviour on one end of the scale to laissez-faire on the other.

The 'gurus' in this area were Kurt Lewin, Robert Tannenbaum, Warren Schmidt and Rensis Likert. Leadership style came into management discussion after Kurt Lewin, Robert Lippitt and R. K. White published their research findings in 1939. They examined the effects of three different leadership styles on a group of boys.

The study found that the authoritarian style stopped initiative and bred hostility, the democratic style promoted a better attitude and the laissez-faire style left the group without direction.

Managing Performance

Figure 2.1 Leadership styles.

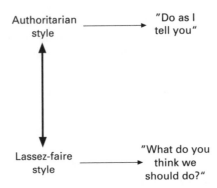

Tannenbaum and Schmidt also viewed leadership as a continuum.

The continuum presents the range of behaviours available to a leader. The behaviour ranged from making decisions on behalf of the followers to involving followers in decision making within organizational constraints. The performance of a leader depended on:

■ personality variables, ability and the expectations of the followers,
■ the leader's personal value system, trust and confidence in the group he or she was leading,
■ his or her preferred leadership style.

Rensis Likert directed leadership studies at the University of Michigan. The objective of these studies was to find out what kinds of organizational structures and what type of leadership behaviour had more impact on employee performance. The studies identified 'employee-oriented' behaviour and 'production-centred' behaviour. The Michigan studies concluded that 'employee-centred' behaviour led to superior performance.

Likert also put forward the following four 'systems of management':

■ System 1: Exploitative–Authoritative. Management is seen as having tight control from the top. There is no trust or confidence in subordinates.
■ System 2: Benevolent–Authoritative. There is a paternalistic attitude from the top. The goals and the decisions are made at the top. The prevailing attitude and behaviour is still that of master–servant.

- System 3: Consultative. The top management decides but there is also consultation with subordinates. There is a reasonable amount of superior–subordinate interaction.
- System 4: Known as System 4. Top management has confidence and trust in subordinates. Decision making is devolved down the hierarchy. Workers are motivated by participation.

Likert advocated System 4 and produced evidence to show that for sustained performance the System 4 approach produced better results than other systems as far as morale and productivity were concerned.

At the same time as the Michigan studies, other leadership studies were being conducted by the Bureau of Business Research at Ohio State University in 1945. The studies picked out two aspects of style which had significance as far as good performance was concerned. These were:

- Consideration: rapport between the leader and his team, trust and concern for his people and a two-way communication.
- Initiating structure: the work is organized, prescriptive and is done as planned.

Their results indicated that morale and performance improved with the consideration approach.

Blake and Moulton adopted a grid approach to combine approaches towards tasks and people.

They asked people to score themselves on a scale from 1–9 on both axes, representing task and people, with 1 representing low concern and 9 high concern.

The grid presented possible leadership styles based on the assumptions made about tasks and people.

The two-dimensional model of Blake and Moulton was adopted and extended by William Reddin into his three-dimensional model.

Reddin's three-dimensional model

Reddin places leadership in various dimensions. The basic leadership style is 'relationship-oriented' or 'task-oriented'. Effective leadership styles are characterized as the developer, executive bureaucrat and benevolent autocrat depending on the given situation.

Contingency theories

All the theorists so far have emphasized the traits and behaviour of leaders. Fred Fiedler in the late 1960s highlighted the role of situational factors. According to Fiedler the appropriate style of leadership was a function of:

- leader–member relations (better relations lead to less use of formal power),
- task structure (routine and repetitive tasks require less freedom),
- position power (higher up in the hierarchy means greater power).

According to Fiedler leadership effectiveness depends on the style adopted depending on situational factors. The more directive style worked best in situations where a leader was liked and trusted by his group, where the task was clear and well defined and where the leader was respected by his group. He also concluded that when the situation was very unfavourable for a leader, again the directive style was needed.

The advantage of this theory is that it fits a lot of practical situations. It also allows leaders to change their style depending on the situations in which they find themselves. Leaders should also keep a 'psychological distance' from their subordinates in order to allow them to change their style of direction when situations demand.

Hersey and Blanchard believe that the best leaders are those who adapt their styles according to various types of people and situations. They believe that there are different ways of influencing and leading people in different situations.

They have developed a Situational Leadership model in deciding what leadership styles are appropriate in different situations. The X axis of the model represents 'task behaviour' and the Y axis 'relationship behaviour'. Using this model leaders can evaluate which style to adopt by analysing individual situations and the level of 'readiness' of their subordinates, i.e. subordinates' willingness and ability to undertake the task. Leaders, depending on given situations have the options to adopt 'delegative' or 'participative' or 'tell' style.

Organizations and leadership training

In order to be effective organizations have relied on various management writers and researchers to come up with definite views on the styles of leadership that are most effective in enhancing organizational performance.

Trait and behaviour theorists have conducted research to provide various views and explanations of leadership styles. Big organizations started using various models in measuring their leadership styles and, of course, many training consultancies developed training in the use of such models. Dr Hersey, for example, claims that his model has been used by "over one million managers at more than five hundred major corporations including General Motors, Rockwell International, IBM, Xerox and Merck".

Leadership in the 1990s

In spite of various researches throughout the century and various models developed by various theorists, there still seems to be a 'leadership vacuum'. In the past decade and in the decade up to the new millennium the business world has changed and will be changing even more dramatically. Understanding the context, global or otherwise (it is said that even small local businesses are now affected by global competition), in which organizations operate and make decisions is very important in understanding the type of leaders that organizations and societies require as we approach the new millennium.

Global competition has accelerated sharply in the past few years. Leaders are required to be conversant with the changing nature of the competitive arena and to lead their organizations to respond to change. In 1958, writing in the *Harvard Business Review* ('Management in the 1980s'), Harold J. Levitt and Thomas L. Whisker, two American professors, predicted that the computer would do to middle management what the Black Death did to fourteenth-century Europeans. So it has; but the impact of computers and technology in general has enabled leaders to transform their organizations radically.

Managing Performance

New technologies and skills are becoming diffused world-wide and businesses are becoming high-tech. The convergence of computing, communications and information will lead to a global information superhighway which will expand markets and intensify global competition.

Everyone is familiar with the Internet and yet a decade ago it was unthinkable that an international network could grow from one million to 30 million users in less than four years. The falling cost of technology and advances in technology have become catalysts in changing the way businesses are being organized.

Politically the climate is changing from conflict to co-operation. The most dramatic change in history has taken place in the geography of capitalism. State-owned businesses are being sold and markets are being liberalized. Privatization and deregulation are becoming the major internal sources of new competition.

Former communist and socialist countries all over the world are opening up their economies and markets and are creating infrastructures to compete with industrially advanced countries. The walls are down and many organizations have assumed borderless operations.

At the business level, leaders have taken initiatives, in some cases out of desperation, to embrace various management thinking and fads that have been put forward by various management 'gurus'. The main objective was to respond to various competitive pressures. They focused their attention on products, processes and people.

In the 1980s most organizations got hooked on Total Quality Management (TQM) in order to achieve and retain competitive advantage. Deming, Juran and Crosby all advocated focus on quality, including quality of leadership. In America the Malcolm Baldrige Award was instituted in 1987 and in Europe the annual European Quality Award was launched in 1992. Both the Baldrige award and the European Award highlighted leadership as one of the key drivers in total quality.

Rank Xerox UK launched a world-wide programme called 'Leadership through Quality' in 1989. Apart from winning various quality awards, the company achieved transformation by focusing attention on management behaviour, training, communication and performance.

Many other companies like ICL, Miliken, Motorola, ABB and so on embraced the total quality management initiative.

Effective leadership

The focus of attention shifted from products to customers. Customer satisfaction became part of the strategy of many organizations.

In 1995 the buzzword which dominated the management world was BPR – Business Process Re-engineering. Hammer and Champy's book *Reengineering the Corporation* became a best-seller as soon as it was published in 1995.

BPR advocated a fundamental rethinking and radical redesign of business processes to achieve a 'quantum leap' in business results. Companies like IBM, Motorola, AT&T, Reuters, Kodak and many others began to look at various activities associated with their core processes, and re-engineered processes by eliminating non-value-adding activities.

Re-engineering led to integration of various tasks and activities and as a result work is performed where it makes most sense. Organizational structures were flattened and technology as an enabler became an important agent of business transformation. Inevitably the re-engineering initiative led to many people losing their jobs and many tasks had to be done by cross-functional teams.

For a long time leaders had to lead organizations that were pyramidal and hierarchical. From the mid-1980s onwards various layers were removed from organizations to make them responsive to customer needs. Organizational agility was the 'management speak' of the time. Power and authority became devolved and 'empowerment' as a management phenomenon became popular and in some cases a business necessity.

Companies like ICL, Motorola, AT&T, BP and so on got themselves into 'empowerment mode'. In 1983 Rosabeth Moss Kanter in her book *The Change Masters – Corporate entrepreneurs at work* emphasized the need for people in organizations to work as 'corporate entrepreneurs'. Due to globalization, intense competition and the opportunity to re-engineer, the time had come to 'empower' employees and devolve decision making throughout organizations. The advocates of empowerment argued that in the de-layered customer-focus organizations where work is done by teams it is important (a) to give employees power to make quick decisions, (b) to get employees' commitment and involvement, and (c) to enable employees to determine their own destiny.

Managing Performance

In 1990 another management 'guru', Peter Senge, published a best-selling book *The Fifth Discipline – the Art & Practice of the Learning Organization*. Learning organizations, according to Senge, are organizations "where people continually expand their capacity to create results they truly desire, where new and expansive patterns of thinking are nurtured, where collective aspiration is set free, and where people are continually learning how to learn together." Senge's theory enjoyed immense popularity.

From being learning organizations and working with empowered, multi-functional teams, organizations now believe that their strategic and competitive advantage lies in leveraging knowledge. The successful corporations of the next millennium will be knowledge-driven, with world-wide information highways, massive computer power and a leadership style that will facilitate value-added by all employees.

According to Peter Drucker:

> ... the modern organization is a destabiliser. It must be organized for innovation ... And it must be organized for the systematic abandonment of whatever is established, customary, familiar and comfortable ... In short it must be organized for constant change. The organization's function is to put knowledge to work ... It is the nature of knowledge that it changes fast and that today's certainties always become tomorrow's absurdities.
>
> Peter Drucker: *Managing in a Time of Change* (1995)

Facing such complexity and market movements, how have 'modern' leaders behaved?

Many leaders got into a downsizing frenzy. 'Re-structuring', 'downsizing, 'right-sizing' and 're-engineering' became synonymous with redundancies. In crises our business leaders have taken a short cut in impressing their masters – their shareholders.

BT numbers fell from 237 400 to 148 900 at the end of March 1995. Barclays' workforce fell below 100 000, with

46

20 000 fewer staff at the end of 1994. In the *Financial Times* in July 1996 the headlines read: 'Philips to shed 6000 jobs'; 'ICI to shed 5000 jobs in two years'. The latest news from ICI came on top of 1400 job losses already in 1996.

BA announced (18 September 1996) that they were going to make 2000 employees redundant due to restructuring.

According to some writers, most leaders operate in a 'cul-de-sac' region when they cannot find a solution. The 'cul-de-sac' refers to their behaviour, their ability, their competence and their values.

How do leaders at the top of organizations justify such actions?

Many management writers and thinkers provide 'psychological rationalization' of leadership action. I have heard some leaders say, "what we are doing is no different to what 'gurus' tell us about business reality". There is no job security now and even writers like Charles Handy write about a 'portfolio of careers'. Such writers provide a micro-universe for leaders to rationalize their actions.

In *Age of Paradox* Charles Handy describes the dark side of today's business. Leaders ruthlessly search for efficiency at the expense of workers.

Some leaders say they are in power to fulfil the expectations of their shareholders. If their businesses are not performing according to the financial expectations of their shareholders (their owners) then they will no longer be in power and will join the ex-heads of IBM, Digital, Kodak, Westinghouse and so on.

In the past few years an interesting debate has emerged as to whether leaders should look after the interests of all their stakeholders (employees, customers, suppliers, shareholders and community). There are two schools of thought on this subject. Some writers argue that the primary focus of attention should be on shareholders because if their expectations are not met then the leaders as well as the employees and other stakeholders will lose out. Also, paying attention to all stakeholders will affect the organization's capabilities to generate good business results. It can also become an excuse for making uncommercial decisions. This debate is revisited later in this book.

Modern writers on leadership

However, modern writers on leadership like **Parikh, Bennis and Kouzes** argue that, whether or not leaders are paying attention to or give equal consideration to all the stakeholders, what matters is the behaviour, values and credibility of leaders. In the book *Beyond Leadership – Balancing Economics, Ethics and Ecology* by Bennis, Parikh and Lessem, Parikh focuses the leader's attention on self-management.

New paradigms highlighted

Parikh advocates a new paradigm for leaders in the late twentieth and twenty-first centuries. He expects modern leaders to break out from their restricted beliefs and ego state. He passionately believes that modern leaders should gain access to and experience higher levels of consciousness and go "beyond ego, thereby opening up alternative, but hitherto dormant, channels of knowing. This is what 'managing your self' in the new paradigm is about." He goes on to say that by adopting this new paradigm modern leaders can perform with 'joy of doing' as opposed to 'fear of losing'.

According to Parikh, assuming 'managing your self' mode will result in peak performance and peak experience.

Once leaders understand themselves, this will enable articulation of a vision statement incorporating values and beliefs everyone can identify with. This approach requires detachment from one's ego. Is this asking too much?. It is said that the true measure of a leader is detachment from his or her ego.

Kouzes and Posner in their book *Credibility* say that "leader credibility is the cornerstone of corporate performance and global competitiveness". Credibility makes a difference. "The six disciplines of credibility – discovering, appreciating, affirming, developing, serving and sustaining – reliably measure actions that build the foundations of leadership; they distinguish between those individuals who can lead others to new visions of the future and those who cannot."

Warren Bennis, a distinguished Professor of Business Administration at the University of Southern California, is considered to be one of the leading 'gurus' on leadership. In his book *On Becoming a Leader* published in 1989 he wrote: "In fact, the process of becoming a leader is much the same as the process of becoming an integrated human being. For the leader, as for any integrated person, life itself is a career . . ."

In the Summer 1996 issue of *Organizational Dynamics* Bennis, in an interview with Richard Hodgetts, says that present leaders face the challenges of globalization and galloping technology. An organization's efforts to improve competitiveness by cutting costs, downsizing, restructuring and re-engineering result in major leadership challenges. An effective leader, according to Bennis, has to generate trust and have a sense of purpose.

The leader has to take account of all the stakeholders and must possess certain values and morals. Self, trust, credibility values (so-called 'soft' issues) are now entering into the analysis of effective leadership.

Leadership: power or responsibility?

Bruce Lloyd, who teaches in the Strategic and International Management Department at South Bank University, London, writes:

> Management books on leadership tend to be preoccupied with power. How to get it, how to use it, and how to keep it. Power, like leadership and management, is usually defined as the ability to make things happen. But increasingly another issue is becoming the focus of the subject: In whose interests are things being made to happen? To be effective in the long term, leadership needs to be more concerned with balancing the interests of the stakeholders in a situation.
>
> Leadership that is purely power-driven will almost inevitably become corrupted; power will be abused. Power-driven leadership is self-focused. An alternative form of leadership is responsibility-driven and *others*-focused.

> A responsibility-driven approach to leadership is inclusive; that is it does not exclusively focus on the interests of one particular group. Power-driven leadership tends to be preoccupied with the short term, while a responsibility approach is more concerned with long-term issues. A responsibility-driven approach is likely to produce a more effective balance of the respective interests of all the various stakeholders, which is essential for the long-term success of any organization. Responsible leadership looks to the future rather than to making a quick return. This is the key to sustainability and success.
>
> (Source: *The Futurist*, May–June 1996)

He goes on to write:

> Responsibilities should not be seen as a burden; they are the vital link that makes organizations and society work, and they are what gives life meaning and purpose. But responsibilities will only be rewarding and effective if they are supported by an overall learning approach to all aspects of life and work. Unfortunately, the willingness to take responsibility, to live with it, and to use and develop it in others is much rarer than it ought to be.
>
> The centre of the debate about leadership needs to be more about how and what we learn about responsibility rather than about power. Leadership needs to be seen as 'the opportunity to exercise responsibility'.
>
> (Source: *The Futurist*, May–June 1996)

Attributes of an ideal leader – What do line managers think?

In 1987 Management Centre Europe, European HQ of the American Management Association, conducted a survey on 'Leadership', asking 1500 European managers to list the attributes of the ideal business leader and match these with their personal impressions of the chief executive they worked for.

Top and middle management executives from all management disciplines and from every country in Europe took part in the poll.

Effective leadership

The respondents believed that the ideal CEO needs the following top qualities:

- The ability to build effective teams
- The ability to listen
- The ability to retain good people
- The ability to surround himself with good people

The true picture that emerged was of "the lonely, strong-willed autocrat (65%) making solo decisions (66%), who is ambitious (65%) and in many cases motivated by power (59%) or money (40%)".

- Fifty-three per cent of respondents said their own CEOs had high ethical standards.
- Only 44 per cent said their CEOs knew how to listen.
- Fifty-nine per cent said their CEOs were motivated by power.
- Forty per cent attributed 'motivated by money' to their own top executives.
- Twenty-eight per cent of CEOs were perceived to be ruthless in their dealings with their people.

James M. Kouzes and Barry Z. Posner, the authors of *Credibility – How Leaders Gain and Lose It, Why People Demand It*, published in 1993, conducted various studies and surveys in order to find out values, characteristics and attitudes that they believed were crucial to leadership.

They highlighted the following leadership characteristics for their surveys:

- Honest
- Forward-looking
- Inspiring
- Competent
- Fair-minded
- Supportive
- Broad-minded
- Intelligent
- Straightforward
- Courageous
- Dependable
- Co-operative

Managing Performance

- Imaginative
- Caring
- Mature
- Determined
- Ambitious
- Loyal
- Self-controlled
- Independent

TIME OUT

From your experience identify five characteristics of a good leader.

1. _____

2. _____

3. _____

4. _____

5. _____

Did you include 'trust' and 'values' in your list?

We have arrived at the situation when markets are changing dramatically and the business environment is becoming 'empowering'. The management language of the 1990s contains the following: empowerment, credibility, knowledge, trust, values, loyalty, teaming, learning, partnerships, responsibility, stakeholders, integrity, 'fat cats', obscene, and so on.

Values

Leadership, we said, was the process of influencing and guiding others. What then is the difference between Gandhi and Hitler, both considered leaders in different situations?

Values are what differentiate 'good' leaders from bad leaders. If you take 'values' away from leaders like Gandhi, Churchill or Eisenhower, you are left with 'leaders' like Hitler and Charles Manson.

Leaders' values should be institutionalized and communicated throughout the organization. There are some CEOs who manage by values. *Business Week* of 12 September 1994 has an article on the management style of Robert D. Hass. Commenting on managing by values Hass, CEO of

Effective leadership

Levi, said: "We are not doing this because it makes us feel good, although it does. We are not doing this because it is politically correct. We are doing this because we believe in the interconnection between liberating the talents of our people and business success."

If the leader and employees share the same values and they internalize these values then the bond between the leader and employees will be stronger. To achieve this a leader has to have a vision of how to meet the interests and expectations of all his or her stakeholders and then to be able to incorporate this vision in formulating business strategy.

In 1992 a survey of executive opinion on 'Corporate Values' was conducted in the United Kingdom by Digital Equipment Co. in association with John Humble. The following table from the survey shows typical relationships between values, vision and strategy.

Trust is another word that has entered management vocabulary, especially in relation to measuring leadership effectiveness. In an article in *The Economist* (6 December 1995) entitled 'Trust in Me', the point is made that organizations are putting more faith in their front-line workers as workers are disappearing and organizations are becoming 'lean'. There is a need for trust.

Typical relationships between values, vision and strategy

Values	Fit with vision and strategies	Capacity and will to adapt	Probable outcome
Strong shared values	Close fit clarity and commitment	High	Positive contribution to economic success High morale and 'ownership'. Quick response to crisis.
Weak confused values	Poor fit Usually confused vision also	Neutral	Organization drifts Poor motivation Uncertainty and ambiguity
Strong shared values	Very poor fit Substantial gap between new vision and strategies and old values		Potential economic disaster Bitter internal conflict between existing value holders and those pressing for changes. Anxiety

(Source: 'Corporate Values – The Bottom Line Contribution'. Digital Equipment Co.)

Managing Performance

The article cites research conducted by two academics at INSEAD, Chan Kim and Renee Mauborgne, who interviewed 3500 managers about the subject of trust. How is trust created in an organization? The only sure way to create trust is to base decisions on 'procedural justice'. Decisions are fair and seen to be fair. There is also a need to involve subordinates in making decisions.

In a climate where jobs are disappearing fast, where there is no job security, and where leaders are paying themselves 'obscene' remuneration it is very difficult for employees to trust their leaders. This is one of the reasons **why some smart companies do dumb things**. Warren Bennis has pointed out that one could get away from trust in a hierarchical command and control type of organization. But in a de-layered and empowered organization trust is very important.

Employees follow their leaders out of intimidation, insecurity, economic necessity and in some cases their perception that 'the boss knows best'. Employees need to follow their leaders because they have trust and faith and perform beyond the call of money.

In an article by Christopher Bartlett and Sumatra Ghoshal, 'Rebuilding Behavioural Context: Turn Process Reengineering into People Rejuvenation' (*Sloan Management Review*, Fall 1995), they write: " . . . most companies that have been able to continually renew themselves have avoided the development of impersonal, distant relationships by building an element best described as trust into their management context. This is the characteristic of an organization that leads people to rely on each other's judgements and depend on each other's commitments."

They go on to write: "Trust is most easily recognized in transparent, open management processes that give employees equity and involvement."

Credibility

There is also a lack of credibility among business leaders today. James O'Toole, professor and one of the leadership 'gurus', said: "Ninety-five per cent of American managers today say the right thing. Five per cent actually do it." Kouzes and Posner in their book *Credibility* say that modern leaders must be trustworthy, have integrity and be inspiring and supportive. Reputation, they say, is human collateral.

Effective leadership

In a book *The Leader of the Future* (The Drucker Foundation) edited by Hesselbein, Goldsmith and Beckard, the authors write: "Leaders of the future will lead because they simply need to. Their *Conviction*, their *Character*, their *Care*, their *Courage*, will drive them to at least try. The people who will lead successfully will be those who can maintain their *Composure* while constantly developing their *Competence* throughout the process. *The Credible* leader will be the leader of the future."

Power

The other aspect of the leadership debate is how leaders exercise power. In an article, 'The Paradox of Power', Bruce Lloyd, Principal Lecturer at South Bank University, writing in *Future View* writes about responsibility-driven leadership: "Responsible leadership looks to the future rather than to making a quick return. That is the real key to sustainability and success. Some power-driven leaders (and organizations) can succeed in the short term, but experience suggests that power-driven individuals invariably contain the seeds of their own destruction based on an apparently infinite need to prove themselves."

Integrity

Jack Welch in one of his interviews said that "a leader should be a good citizen." Over 40 years ago Peter Drucker wrote:

The best practices will fail to build the right spirit unless management bears witness for its own professional beliefs every time it appoints a man to a management job. The final proof of its sincerity and seriousness is uncompromising emphasis on integrity of character. For it is character through which leadership is exercised, it is character that sets the example and it is imitated in turn . . . They may forgive a man a great deal: incompetence, ignorance, insecurity or bad manners. But they will not forgive his lack of integrity.

Peter Drucker: *Practice of Management* (1955).

Snapshots of conversations with some modern leaders

Author: "What do you think of the present debate on leadership?"

Conversation 1

Leader: "I agree with your point about how a leader should trust his employees and have values and integrity and all that. This is what I would want to do but my leadership is based on what I have to do. In my case I am the managing director of a small private company. I have to impress my board and do what they expect me to do. If I adopt a 'soft' approach my employees will misunderstand me."

Conversation 2

Leader: "I manage a multi-million pound company. There is no way I would risk my job and my company by putting hundred per cent faith on employees. My first priority and loyalty is to my board and my shareholders. Growth and margins are the main drivers of performance. Once we achieve these we can then pay attention to our employees.

"Our benefits scheme is very good and, in my view, benefits and money motivate people. My values and character do not matter as long as I keep City analysts happy and shareholders receive good dividends."

Conversation 3

Leader: "I did believe in balancing the interests of all stakeholders when I was the CEO of an engineering company. We lost market share and I was accused of indecision and bad decisions. I have now learnt my lessons. If you can achieve financial targets and focus your attention on short-term results you will survive in this cut-throat world."

Comments: These leaders will achieve success in the short term. They need to transform themselves at a personal level, examining the values they hold and their level of integrity and trust. Personal transformation will lead to corporate transformation which in turn will result in sustained high performance. At present these leaders work on 'hit and run' principles.

Pygmalion effect

Professor J. Sterling Livingston of Harvard University asserted that leaders who have confidence in their ability to develop and stimulate followers to higher levels of performance will treat them with confidence and self-esteem. Such leaders exert positive influence and obtain better results.

Leadership for the new millennium

In the report on 'Developing leadership for the 21st century' published by the Economist Intelligence Unit in 1996, the following yardsticks for measuring leadership effectiveness are highlighted for different time periods, 'today', 'in 10 years' and in the 'future':

Today

Profitability
Customer satisfaction
Sustained growth

In 10 years

Customer satisfaction
Long-term return to investors
Profitability

Future
North America

Long-term shareholder value
Customer satisfaction
Bottom-line responsibility

Managing Performance

Europe

Customer satisfaction
Bottom-line responsibility
Long-term shareholder value

Asia

Customer satisfaction
Bottom-line responsibility
Long-term shareholder value

Latin America

Customer satisfaction
Sustained growth
Long-term shareholder value

(Source: 'Developing leadership for the 21st century'. Written in co-operation with Korn/Ferry International. EIU. 1996)

TIME OUT

Measure the effectiveness of your leader (your supervisor, your team leader, your manager, your CEO).
Award 1 point for yes and 2 points for 'no'.

1. Is he an insulated leader?
2. Has he spoken to you?
3. Is he competent in what he does?
4. Do you know what his values are?
5. Has he communicated his values to his employees in the whole organization?
6. Can you trust him?
7. Does he trust you?
8. Is he fair in his dealings with customers, employees, suppliers etc.?
9. Is he supportive in times of crisis?
10. Does he consider himself as a 'servant' to others?
11. Do people inside and outside the organization respect him?
12. Does he understand the nature of competition and the market?
13. Does he treat you with dignity and respect?

Effective leadership

14. Is he ruthless?
15. Does he project a macho image?
16. Is he a good communicator?
17. Does he listen?
18. Is he honest?
19. Does he stimulate people to gain new competencies and skills?
20. Does he lead by example?

SCORING

Score 23 points: You are lucky. You have a trustworthy, inspiring and future-oriented leader.

22–26. You have a good leader.

27–31. You have a fair leader.

32–37. I am sorry. You have an 'empty suit' leader. He looks good and maybe makes all the right noises but he is devoid of consideration, values, respect for others and integrity.

In the future when you look at your or any other company's accounts and assess their assets and liabilities, do also prepare a 'leadership' balance sheet for that company.

Leadership Balance Sheet

Assets	Return on assets £	Liabilities	Cost of liabilities £
Honesty		Greed	
Integrity		Macho	
Communication		Ruthless	
Competence		Completely numbers-oriented	
Appreciation		Short-term	
Consideration		Insulated	
Trustworthy		Arrogance	
Trusting		No vision	
Caring		Lack of innovation	
Supportive		Fearful	
Passion for customers		Uninspiring	
Credible		Scandals	
Recognition		Manipulator	
Respect		Control freak	

Put a monetary value on each asset and each liability. Valuation is subjective. Cost out to find to what extent liability cost exceeds asset returns.

Good news and bad news on leadership effectiveness

Bad news first:

- There are still many organizations who believe that good leadership involves being ruthless and intimidating workers in doing their jobs.
- Much leadership training is still based on the styles approach.
- Myers-Briggs, Belbin, Blake and Moulton and other instruments which are used in leadership training show you how you are now. They do not provide guidance on how you should be.
- There is very little training, if any, available on 'teaching' being courageous, credible and honest.
- Some leaders still believe their first consideration is towards their shareholders.
- There is no interest on the part of the leaders in understanding themselves.

Good news:

- Many writers are now writing books and articles on leadership emphasizing the importance of trust and values.
- There is much awareness now among corporate leaders in truly empowering their employees and working as a team.
- Leaders leading organizations like Motorola and Unipart are putting their money where their mouths are in truly balancing the interests and expectations of all stakeholders.
- Changing business circumstances and 'lean' organizations will force the leaders of the twenty-first century to behave like a leader and not a boss.

Are you a 'boss' or a leader?

A boss creates fear	**A leader creates confidence**
'Bossism' breeds resentment	**Leadership breeds enthusiasm**
A boss says 'I'	**A leader says 'we'**
A boss fixes blame	**A leader fixes mistakes**
A boss knows how	**A leader shows how**
'Bossism' makes work drudgery	**Leadership makes work interesting**
A boss relies on authority	**A leader relies on co-operation**
A boss drives	**A leader leads**
Source: Unknown	

Selected reading

Bartlett, C. A. and Goshal, S. (1995). Rebuilding Behavioural Context: Turn Process Reengineering into People Rejuvenation. *Sloan Management Review*, Fall.

Hesselbein, F., Goldsmith, M. and Beckhard, R. (1996). *The Leader of the Future*. Jossey-Bass Publishers.

Kouzes, J. M. and Posner, B. Z. (1987). *The Leadership Challenge*. Jossey-Bass Publishers.

Kouzes, J. M. and Posner, B. Z. (1993). *Credibility*. Jossey-Bass Publishers.

Drucker, P. (1955). *The Practice of Management*. Butterworth-Heinemann.

Wild, R. (1994). *How To Manage*. Butterworth-Heinemann.

Hodgetts, R. (1996). A Conversation with Warren Bennis on Leadership in the Midst of Downswing. *Organizational Dynamics*, Summer.

Semler, R. (1993). *Maverick*. Century.

The Economist Intelligence Unit. (1996). Developing leadership for the 21st. century.

Stewart, T. A. (1993). Welcome to the Revolution. *Fortune*, 13 December.

Bennis, W., Parikh, J. and Lessem, R. (1994). *Beyond Leadership – Balancing Economics, Ethics and Ecology*. Blackwell.

3

Financial performance

in brief

Financial statements are like fine perfume; to be sniffed but not swallowed.
Unknown

Summary

■ Over a very long time organizations have focused their attention on financial indicators to monitor and measure performance.

■ Financial information is categorized into Balance Sheet, Profit & Loss Account and Sources and Application of Funds. Different sets of accounts generate different information in relation to the trading position, assets and liabilities of a business.

■ From these accounts different ratios are prepared to monitor the operations of different businesses or divisions.

■ In the late 1980s and early 1990s emphasis was put on Activity-Based Costing (ABC) in order to enhance organizational performance. The practice of assigning costs to products according to the demands each product made on the company's overhead resources was adopted.

■ In the past few years analysts have focused their attention on how managers use shareholders' funds. In response to enhancing shareholder value different consultancies have engaged in marketing battleplans to present their concepts and models of measuring shareholder value.

■ Monetary Value Added, Economic Value Added and Cashflow Return on Investment are presented as providing the answers. MVA, EVA and Cashflow ROI have become the business clichés of the late 1990s.

Financial performance

Financial performance reflects how an organization is controlling and monitoring its corporate objectives and its operations. After all, many organizations in the private sector exist to make a profit. Without profit, shareholders' return will be non-existent and the company will go into liquidation. The organization, therefore, owes it to its shareholders and employees to remain solvent and to achieve the financial objectives set in its plan.

Origins of financial accounting

According to H. Thomas Johnson and Robert S. Kaplan (in their book entitled *Relevance Lost – The Rise and Fall of Management Accounting*) financial reports have been prepared for thousands of years. The demand for keeping financial records has existed since trade began.

However, the need for management accounting as such came into existence as a consequence of the Industrial Revolution as a new type of organization (the 'managed organization') came into being. This type of organization brought about the divorce between ownership and control. Thus was born the profession of manager and the need for recording transactions occurring within the organization.

For a number of years the accounting system was merely designed to accommodate keeping information on transactions. The system was not used to assess the performance of an organization.

Gradually, with the development of department stores and retail chains, these organizations improved their accounting system in order to measure internal and external performance.

The system developed with the introduction of a scientific management system and a hierarchical organizational structure. According to Johnson and Kaplan the most innovative system was the return on investment (ROI) measure which provided an overall assessment of commercial success. "By 1925 virtually all management accounting practices used today had been developed."

Sources of financial information

There are three sources of financial information for organizations in the private sector. These are the Balance Sheet, Profit & Loss Account and Sources and Application of Funds.

1 Balance Sheet

A Balance Sheet is a financial situation showing what a company owes (its liabilities) and what it owns (its assets). It is a statement of the total assets and liabilities of a business at a particular moment of time. In other words, it is a financial snapshot of the business.

Assets include debtors, stock (current assets) and machinery, buildings and plant (fixed assets).

Liabilities include creditors, bank overdraft and taxation.

2 Profit & Loss Account

The second source of information is the Profit & Loss Account. It shows how the company has traded in the year it is reporting. The account includes revenue and expenditure items which relate to the year under consideration and these items are matched to calculate profit or loss. Profit is the excess of sales revenue over the costs incurred in achieving that sales revenue.

3 Sources and Application of Funds

The third source of information is Sources and Application of Funds. This tells us where the money in the business has come from (issue of shares, borrowing, etc.) and how it has been spent or applied (investment in fixed assets and working capital).

Analysing financial ratios

Many financial indicators in themselves do not give information on the health of a company. If, however, these indicators are compared with other indicators and presented as a ratio then they begin to tell a story in relation to the performance of a company or a division.

We shall now examine the key financial ratios used in a private sector enterprise.

Return on capital employed (ROCE)

$$\frac{\text{Profit}}{\text{Capital employed}}$$

Capital employed is total assets minus current assets.
Profit is operating profit or profit before interest and tax.

ROCE tells us how management has used the total funds available to the business; it measures its earning power. Value is only added to the business if it earns a higher ROCE than the rate of interest it pays or would pay on borrowings.

ROCE is influenced by profit margin and asset turnover. Profit margin and asset turnover tend to vary inversely. The combined effect of profit margin and asset turnover is very important in achieving return on investment.

Profit margin

Gross trading profit equals sales revenue minus cost of sales.

$$\text{Profit margin \% equals} \quad \frac{\text{Profit before interest and tax}}{\text{Sales (turnover)}}$$

Asset turnover

$$\text{Asset turnover is} \quad \frac{\text{Sales}}{\text{Capital employed}}$$

The figure shows the frequency with which assets have been converted into sales during the accounting period.

Return on assets (ROA)

The product of profit margin and asset turnover is known as Return on Assets.

ROA equals profit margin $\times$ asset turnover.

ROA equals

$$\frac{\text{Profit before tax and interest}}{\text{Sales}} \times \frac{\text{Sales}}{\text{Assets}} = \frac{\text{Profit before tax and interest}}{\text{Assets}}$$

ROA measures profit as a percentage of total assets.

Return on equity (ROE)

$$\text{ROE equals} \quad \frac{\text{Profit after tax}}{\text{Shareholders' funds}}$$

This ratio, to use an American expression, 'measures bang per buck'. It involves managing profit margin, asset turnover and financial leverage.

ROE is influenced by timing (distorted if a company has just undertaken heavy start-up costs), risk (does not reflect the degree of risk undertaken) and value. It reflects book value rather than market value.

From the Balance Sheet one can also measure stock turnover, debtor turnover, creditor turnover, liquidity ratios and gearing ratio.

Stock turnover

$$\text{Stock turnover equals} \quad \frac{\text{Sales}}{\text{Stock}}$$

This ratio shows how quickly stock is converted into sales.

Debtor days

$$\text{Debtor days equal} \quad \frac{\text{Debtors}}{\text{Cost of sales}} \times 365$$

This gives an indication of the number of days' sales for which payment is outstanding.

Creditor days

$$\text{Creditor days equal } \frac{\text{Trade creditors}}{\text{Cost of sales}} \times 365$$

This gives an indication of the number of days' purchases for which payment is still due. Credit taken from suppliers is a source of short-term finance.

The acid ratio

$$\text{The acid ratio equals } \frac{\text{Debtors} + \text{Cash}}{\text{Current liabilities}}$$

This shows the organization's ability to finance its immediate liabilities.

The current ratio

$$\text{The current ratio equals } \frac{\text{Current assets}}{\text{Current liabilities}}$$

This shows what resources are available to meet liabilities.

Gearing ratio

$$\text{Gearing ratio equals } \frac{\text{Total debt}}{\text{Shareholders' funds}} \times 100$$

This gives an indication of the company's ability to finance its operations in the long run.

Financial performance highlighted so far falls under the categories of profitability, solvency and financial structure (Figure 3.1).

Profitability	Solvency	Financial structure
Return on capital employed	Acid test	Debt-to-assets ratio
Return on investment	Current ratio	Debt-to-equity ratio
Return on equity	Stocks	
Profit margin	Current assets	

Figure 3.1 Categories of financial performance

Managing working capital

Current assets minus current liabilities gives information on the working capital. The management of working capital is the lifeblood of any business. Profits do not equal cash. Timely conversion of cash into inventories, accounts receivable and back to cash is the lifeblood of any company. An organization becomes profitable by selling its goods and services but if not enough cash is flowing in to meet its obligations it becomes insolvent. **Performance must focus on cash flows as well as profits**.

In Figure 3.2 cash is locked in for 110 days, that is, nearly four months. The size of the net figure for working capital has a direct effect on the liquidity of a company. The return on capital employed is also affected by the level of working capital. The higher the investment in working capital, the lower will be the return on capital employed.

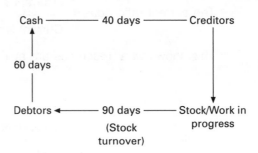

Figure 3.2 Working capital cycle

Finally, as far as financial measures are concerned there are also measures from a stock market perspective. These are the price/earnings ratio and earnings per share.

Price/earnings ratio (PE Ratio)

$$\frac{\text{Price per share}}{\text{Earnings per share}}$$

The PE ratio tells us something about current financial performance. It is a useful indicator of how shareholders feel about the company's future prospects.

Earnings per share (EPS)

Earnings per share equal $\dfrac{\text{Earnings}}{\text{The number of ordinary shares issued}}$

EPS is used by many analysts as an indicator of corporate performance.

Dividend yield

Dividend yield equals $\dfrac{\text{Dividends per share}}{\text{Market price per share}}$

This indicates an investor's current income yield in relation to the share's current market price.

Dividend cover

Dividend cover equals $\dfrac{\text{Earnings per share}}{\text{Dividends per share}}$

This measures the number of times that the dividend could have been paid out of the current year's earnings.

Get an annual report of your company and try to calculate some of these ratios to get a sense of its financial performance.

Calculate:

1. Return on capital: $\dfrac{\text{Profit after tax}}{\text{Shareholders' funds}}$

2. Return on assets: $\dfrac{\text{Profit before tax and interest}}{\text{Assets}}$

3. Profit margin: $\dfrac{\text{Profit before tax and interest}}{\text{Sales (Turnover)}}$

Managing Performance

4. Net asset turnover:
$$\frac{\text{Sales}}{\text{Net assets}}$$

5. Fixed asset turnover:
$$\frac{\text{Sales}}{\text{Fixed assets}}$$

6. Stock turnover:
$$\frac{\text{Sales}}{\text{Stocks}}$$

7. Debtor turnover:
$$\frac{\text{Sales}}{\text{Debtors}}$$

8. Creditor turnover:
$$\frac{\text{Sales}}{\text{Creditors}}$$

9. The acid ratio:
$$\frac{\text{Liquid assets (Debtors + Cash)}}{\text{Current liabilities}}$$

10. Current ratio:
$$\frac{\text{Current assets}}{\text{Current liabilities}}$$

11. Gearing ratio:
$$\frac{\text{Total debt}}{\text{Shareholders' funds}} \times 100$$

12. Earnings per share:
$$\frac{\text{Profit after tax}}{\text{Number of ordinary shares issued}}$$

13. Price/earnings ratio:
$$\frac{\text{Market price per share (see newspaper)}}{\text{Earnings per share}}$$

14. Dividend yield:
$$\frac{\text{Dividend per share}}{\text{Market price per share}}$$

15. Dividend cover:
$$\frac{\text{Earnings per share}}{\text{Dividends per share}}$$

Financial performance

Ratios   Comments on performance

1. _____
   _____
   _____

2. _____
   _____
   _____

3. _____
   _____
   _____

4. _____
   _____

5. _____
   _____
   _____

6. _____
   _____
   _____

7. _____
   _____
   _____

8. _____
   _____
   _____

9. _____
   _____

10. _____
    _____
    _____

11. _____
    _____
    _____

12. _____
    _____

13. _____
    _____
    _____

14. _____
    _____
    _____

15. _____
    _____

Managing Performance

CAUTION

- The ratios are only as accurate as the figures from which they are calculated.
- Before comparing and interpreting ratios consider the methods used in formulating these figures.
- Ratios by themselves do not tell the whole story.
- Compare like with like.
- Go behind the ratios to assess true performance.

Activity-based costing and cost performance

In the late 1980s Robert Kaplan and Robin Cooper, both professors at Harvard Business School, advocated adoption of Activity-Based Costing (ABC) in order to focus attention on cost behaviour with a view to reducing unit cost per cost driver. The main objective of ABC was to assign costs to products according to the demands each product made on the company's resources.

The adoption of ABC involves two distinctive steps:

1. (a) Identify a relatively small set of cost drivers. (For example, the cost driver for material handling will be product-line lengths and the appropriate measurement will be feet/assembly line. Or the cost driver for set-up will be duration and the measurement will be average set-up time.)

   (b) Trace indirect cost to each driver.
2. The company should determine the percentage of drivers consumed by each product or service.

The outcome: an estimate of the indirect costs of each product or service based on such drivers.

Activities are tasks that people or machines perform in order to provide a product or service to a customer. In other words, activity is a particular process of doing something, generally involving a number of steps or operations.

Adopting ABC resulted in eliminating non-value-adding processes and activities. The philosophy behind ABC was similar to the one adopted by Business Process Re-engineering, which was to focus attention on activities and processes with a view to slimlining processes and eliminating non-value-adding activities and processes.

According to Peter Drucker:

> Traditional cost accounting in manufacturing – now seventy-five years old, does not record the cost of non-producing, such as the cost of faulty quality, or of a machine being out of order, or of needed parts not being on hand. Yet these unrecorded and uncontrolled costs in some plants run as high as the costs that traditional accounting does record. By contrast, a new method of cost accounting developed in the past ten years – called 'activity based' accounting – records all costs. And it relates them, as traditional cost accounting cannot, to value added. Within the next ten years it should be in general use.

Peter Drucker (1995). *Managing In a Time of Great Change.* Butterworth-Heinemann

Performance measures: *The Sunday Times/*Braxton Associates survey

A *Sunday Times* survey in conjunction with Braxton Associates, a firm of management consultants, found that:

- Earnings per share (EPS) is used by many corporations as an indicator of corporate performance.
- Most companies still use EPS as an indicator to guide their business.
- Forty-five per cent of those surveyed (125 respondents out of 200 companies) said EPS was a key determinant of share price.
- When asked "What do you believe are the drivers of your company's share price?" there was the following response:

    1. Earnings growth (70%)
    2. Dividend growth (54%)
    3. Earnings per share (45%)
    4. Cash flow statement (33%)
    5. Price/earnings (15%)

Managing Performance

- When asked " What are the principal measures used to monitor the performance?" the response was:

  1. Meeting strategic targets (70%)
  2. RONA/ROCE (58%)
  3. Growth (50%)
  4. Cashflow return on investment (42%)
  5. Return on sales (38%)
     (Source: *The Sunday Times*, 11 August 1996)

Financial measures still dominate and preoccupy many organizations. According to the Economist Intelligence Unit's research conducted in association with KPMG (1994), most companies still track profits, earnings per share and growth in sales as key performance indicators of their businesses. The same report concludes that 70 per cent of the respondents feel dissatisfied with the company's performance system.

Corporate Rituals and Financial Monitoring

The following case study is taken from the book *Total Management Thinking* written by the author.

Case Study: Company 'A'

Company 'A' is a publishing company based in London and New York. Its annual sales turnover is £50 million. The company is divided into four product divisions: Science, Social Sciences, Business Management and Arts. In addition it has acquired a small training business which provides public and in-company seminars on taxation.

Ritual No. 1: Preparing to submit the budget

In December each year all divisions are asked to submit the business goals of their divisions for the following year and the subsequent two years. By mid-January the divisions have to submit the complete budget showing all sources of revenue and all costs. Before the preparation of budgets the Managing Director analyses the actual financial performance of all divisions and then sets the revenue, gross margin and net margin targets. This is known as setting performance targets by extrapolation. No attempt is made to go **behind the figures** to understand actual performance.

Before submission of their respective budgets by mid January all divisional heads have to key in all the revenue and cost figures in detail on the spreadsheets while the accounting department staff keep themselves busy calculating overhead items such as occupancy, headquarters staff cost etc.

Ritual No. 2: Forecasting

In May the first quarter forecasting meeting is held between the Managing Director, Divisional Head, Financial controllers and Finance Director. The budget is analysed to see if it is on track and variances are discussed. If there are significant variances the Managing Director requires a full explanation and an action plan, especially if there are unfavourable variances. Considerable pressure is put on all Divisional heads to get back on track.

In August and again in November forecasting meetings are held and the Divisional heads go through the same hoops as in May.

Ritual No. 3: Monthly analysis

In between forecasting all Divisional heads have to produce monthly analyses of their business. These are co-ordinated by the financial controllers and submitted to the management committee which meets every month.

Ritual No. 4: Staff appraisals

Company 'A' values its staff and they have a system of appraising staff performance every March. Each Divisional Manager is asked to appraise all his or her staff. There is no standard format and the managers do not have to submit their reports to the Personnel Department. Most managers consider appraising their staff as a chore and time-consuming.

Conclusion and comments

Company 'A' to some extent is a 'command and control' type company. If you have not achieved the budget prescribed by the Managing Director and the Management Committee you have underperformed. No attempt is made to analyse actual performance by going behind the figures and examining the market situation.

In addition to financial performance this company should pay attention to other dimensions of performance as well. Because at the moment the company is achieving all its financial targets they feel they must be doing something right!

A true measure of performance

A company producing micro-chips recently gave a high incentive bonus to the division that did not meet its budget. Two other divisions exceeded the budget. The Chief Executive Officer of this company explained to all divisions that the division that did not meet its budget had undergone considerable external pressures which were not foreseen at the time of submitting the budget, and they worked very hard and smart and performed magnificently to bring about achievement, which they did. The company wanted to say 'thank you' to that division. This Chief Financial Officer has the right measure of performance!

Drucker on new measurements

Balance sheets were designed to show what a business would be worth if liquidated today. Budgets are meant to ensure that money is spent only where authorized. What managements need, however, are balance sheets that relate the enterprise's current condition to its future wealth-producing capacity, both short term and long term. Managements need budgets that relate proposed expenditures to future results but also provide follow-up information that shows whether promised results have actually been achieved.

So far, we have only bits and pieces; the cash-flow forecast, for example, or the analysis of proposed capital investments. Now, however, for the first time, some large multinational companies – American and European – are beginning to put these pieces together into 'going-concern' balance sheets and 'going-concern' budgets.

But most needed – and totally lacking – are measurements to give us business control. Financial accounting, balance sheets, profit-and-loss statements, allocation of costs, and so forth are an X-ray of the enterprise's skeleton. But much as the diseases we most commonly die from – heart disease, cancer, Parkinson's – do not show up in a skeleton X-ray, a loss of market standing or a failure to innovate does not register in the accountant's figures until the damage has been done.

We need new measurements – call them a 'business audit' – to give us effective business control . . . But at least we know now that we need new measurements, and we know what they have to be. Slowly, and still gropingly, we are moving away from counting to measuring.

Peter Drucker (1995). *Managing in a Time of Great Change*

A new perspective of corporate performance

In the past decade many organizations have de-layered their structures, re-engineered their processes, innovated their products and empowered their employees in order to improve their organizational performance. The bottom line of all these new approaches has been to get close to their customers in order to materialize their strategic objectives.

These new initiatives also included the search for new measures which were in alignment with their corporate strategies and goals. The balanced scorecard approach (which we will consider later on) is one of the approaches adopted. However, many consultants have also advocated a value-based approach to performance measurement and management.

Creating shareholders' value has become a mantra for many top management because they believe that the ultimate aim of a business is to generate value for its shareholders in the form of financial returns. Many companies try to relate shareholders' interests to their employees' interests by tying financial performance to employee performance.

Managing Performance

In an article, 'What is value-based management?', which appeared in *The McKinsey Quarterly*, 1994, No. 1, the author Timothy Koller puts forward Value-Based Management (VBM) as a measurement metric: "The value of the company is determined by the discounted future cash flows. Value is created only when companies invest capital at returns that exceed the cost of that capital." VBM focuses on key drivers of value. It involves managing the balance sheet as well as the income statement, and balancing long- and short-term perspectives.

To be effective all organizations have to align their corporate objectives to divisional objectives, and their management processes and performance measurement systems, including staff performance and incentive scheme, to value creation.

To focus on VBM companies need to set goals in terms of discounted cash flow value and these goals should be translated into short- and long-term targets. In addition, other dimensions incorporating non-financial objectives such as employee and customer satisfaction should also be considered.

The focus on discounted cashflow valuation can transform organizational decision making and performance.

Do you care enough for your shareholders?

In recent years there has been a growing popularity of two performance measurement methods: Economic Value Added and Market Value Added. This is due to increased interest in focusing attention on shareholders and on the principle of shareholder value.

Economic Value Added (EVA)

EVA is presented as a new theory of corporate performance. It measures how management has increased or decreased the value of capital that shareholders have given it. It is calculated as after-tax net operating profit minus cost of capital. A positive EVA signifies an increase in the value of capital for shareholders.

Financial performance

The concepts of Market Value Added (MVA) and EVA were developed by Stern Stewart & Co., the New York management consultants. In an article, 'Creating Stockholder Wealth', by Anne B. Fisher which appeared in *Fortune* on 11 December 1995, she explains MVA as "a measure of the wealth a company has created for investors. MVA in effect shows the difference between what investors put in and what they can take out." According to Bennett Stewart, a senior partner of Stern Stewart, EVA "shines a light on all four ways wealth can be created in business: by cutting costs, by investing in value-added endeavours, by releasing capital imprisoned in underperforming activities and by reducing the cost of capital."

Market Value Added (MVA)

"To arrive at MVA Stewart adds up all the capital a company has acquired from equity and debt offerings, bank loans, and retained earnings over its life span. The consultants make further adjustments, such as capitalizing R&D spending as an investment in future earnings and amortizing it over an appropriate period. The final tally is then contrasted with the current value of the company's stock and debt. The difference between total market value and invested capital is MVA."

In December 1996 *The Sunday Times* published the Market Value Added of the 200 UK quoted companies: 'Top 100 companies – the winners and the losers'. The 1996 Top 10 MVA winners were Shell, Glaxo Wellcome, SmithKline Beecham, Unilever, BAT, BP, Reuters, Marks & Spencer, BSkyB and Zeneca. The bottom 10 companies were British Steel, Hanson, Trafalgar Square, ICI, Signet, Cordiant, Tarmac, BAe, Arjo Wiggins Appleton and Ladbroke.

MVA is supposed to be a good performance indicator of whether the companies have made money for their shareholders or not. MVA embodies the market expectations, hence the concept involves a forward-looking approach.

"EVA, on the other hand, is after-tax net operating profit minus cost of capital. A positive EVA often signifies a strong stock."

The following companies have pioneered the measurement of MVA and EVA:

Managing Performance

Coca Cola	Tenneco
AT&T	Burton
Quaker Oats	Lucas-Varity
Eli Lilly	

EVA also has an impact on employees' performance and behaviour. The measurement of EVA is tied to the performance bonus. Precautions are taken to avoid manipulation of EVA and the calculation of the bonus. It is a measure of aligning shareholders' objectives to employees' objectives.

CFROI

This is cashflow return on investment which is gaining popularity among many organizations. Many analysts like this performance indicator of business performance. CFROI measures how much cashflow is generated compared to capital investment. In other words, it measures managers' efforts in achieving returns from the capital which is entrusted to them.

How to use financial measures effectively

- Gain an understanding of the components of the balance sheet and profit & loss statements.
- Work out different financial ratios and understand what they mean.
- Determine which indicators to use, bearing in mind the time span involved.
- Financial indicators and measures are a matter of horses for courses. Choose the measures that are appropriate to your business.
- Financial measures must be supported by other measures to gain a comprehensive performance picture.

Performance measures should be coherent with corporate strategy.

Look at the financial reports of your organization and examine the financial measures used. Do you think they are coherent with your corporate strategy?

TIME OUT

_____

_____

_____

_____

_____

_____

Selected reading

CFO Magazine (1996). Keeping Score: Where Strategy & Performance Metrics Meet. October.

Fortune (1996). Eli Lilly is making shareholders rich. How? By linking pay to EVA. 9 September.

Higgins, R. C. (1995). _Analysis For Financial Management_. Dow-Jones Irwin.

Johnson, T. and Kaplan, R. (1987). _Relevance Lost. The Rise and Fall of Management Accounting_.

Koller, T. (1994). What is value-based management? _The McKinsey Quarterly_, No. 3.

Lynn, M. (1996). How best to measure performance. _The Times_, 11 August.

The Sunday Times (1996). 'Playing With Numbers'. 14 July.

Jackson, T. (1996). How EVA measures up. _The Financial Times_, 7 October.

Measuring employees' performance

in brief

Whatever you say, words without deeds are futile and useless.
Aeschylus, 'Prometheus Bound'

Summary

■ Every organization has the responsibility of measuring the performance of its employees. Appraising the performance of employees is a must.

■ Appraisals should be linked with organizational strategy. This necessitates the communication of organizational strategy and objectives throughout the organization.

■ Most managers do not like to appraise their staff because they find the whole thing a chore and time-consuming.

■ Focus on performance is not a phenomenon of the 1990s. Throughout the century various management writers have come up with various theories and systems to measure workers' performance.

■ Some pioneers like Frank Taylor were interested in boosting productivity and finding ways of maximizing workers' efforts. Others, like Maslow, were more interested in exploring the causes of motivation at work.

Measuring employees' performance

■ From the 1960s onwards various writers have put forward theories and methods of measuring employees' performance. These included the Behaviourally Anchored Rating System (BARS) and Graphic Rating Scales.

■j Formulating appraisal systems involves (a) identifying and clarifying corporate objectives and departmental objectives, (b) thinking about job dimensions, (c) categorizing key tasks and highlighting key results areas (KRAs), and (d) devising a measuring scale.

■ All employees should be involved in formulating the objectives of their appraisals. This will create ownership and the appraisals will be perceived to be fair and open. After all, the person who knows the job best is the one doing it.

■ All employees should conduct their own appraisal (self-assessment).

■ Appraisals should not be seen as regular corporate rituals everyone has to go through but as a pleasant, useful and meaningful experience to look forward to.

■ The 360-degree feedback system is gaining popularity among many organizations. Such a system embraces the views of all appropriate direct stakeholders.

■ The 360-degree feedback system is used at Federal Express and W. H. Smith Group plc.

■ American research on designing an effective 360-degree appraisal feedback system. Identification of main components of the system and the summary of the research results.

■ Performance is a function of (a) knowing what to do (job clarification), (b) knowing how to do it (job skills), (c) wanting to do it (motivation) and (d) being able to do it (support, counselling, coaching and mentoring).

Employees are one of the major stakeholders for every organization, both commercial and not-for-profit organizations. Employees give the best part of their lives to organizations. There is, therefore, a 'moral' obligation to let them know how they are performing. At the same time organizations have to measure the performance of all their resources. Unlike technology and capital, this resource (people) has expectations and interests and they are manifested in behaviour which impacts performance.

Appraising and measuring employees' performance involve economic, sociological and psychological perspectives. All these perspectives have been adopted by different management theorists and writers at different periods of management history.

Early pioneers

Economic perspective and Frederick Taylor – The father of scientific management

Economics is about using scarce resources efficiently and effectively. Labour (employees) is one of the scarce resources. The demand for labour is derived demand; this means the demand for labour is derived from the demand for goods and service it produces.

From an economic perspective, the focus on measurement is on productivity, i.e. output per person per hour. This was also the approach adopted by Frederick Taylor who is regarded as the father of scientific management. He developed the theory of one best way. His philosophy was that there is one best way to perform every job. The manager's job should be planning work and the subordinate's job implementing or doing. He conducted several experiments and studies on work measurement and output.

Taylor set out to determine scientifically what workers ought to be able to do with their equipment and materials in order to improve their performance. He put forward the following principles:

■ Use scientific method in planning each job, formulating clearly stated rules and principles and thus avoiding rule-of-thumb methods.
■ Workers should be selected on the basis of their suitability, physically and mentally, to give their best efforts.
■ Motivation through bonuses and incentives should be used to improve output.
■ The task should be divided between planning and implementation. The manager should plan and the workers should be involved in 'doing'.

■ The manager should concern himself only with 'excep-
tions' thus "leaving him free to consider broader lines of
policy and to study the character and fitness of the men
under him" (Frederick Taylor: *Shop Management*, 1903)

Taylor was seriously concerned with industrial output and
workers' performance. His methods became very popular
and had significant impact for years.

Beside Taylor there were other management thinkers who
were also interested in work planning, measurement and
performance. They included:

■ Henry L. Gantt who designed a work scheduling system
using a chart which became known as a Gantt chart and
is still used in many work situations.
■ Frank and Lilian Gilbreth who created an understanding
of motion study and the importance of increasing output
by economizing on physical efforts.
■ Henri Fayol, a French mining engineer, who became
interested in examining an effective performance of
managerial tasks. He concerned himself with developing
management principles. He presented management
functions as being planning, organizing, commanding
and controlling.

In the first quarter of the twentieth century the quest was for
industrial improvement by effectively adopting principles of
scientific management.

Human relations approach and performance

In the second quarter of the twentieth century behavioural
scientists focused their attention on the importance of human
relations and their impact on workers' performance. Among
the well-known pioneers in this area were Elton Mayo,
Abraham Maslow, Douglas McGregor and Frederick
Herzberg.

Elton Mayo led a group of social scientists and industrial
psychologists to study how employees reacted to incentives,
rest periods and job design. The Hawthorne study became

well known among management students. The study was conducted in the early 1920s at the Hawthorne Plant of the Western Electric Company in Illinois, USA. The study lasted for three years.

The Hawthorne study highlighted the following:

- Social and psychological interactions in the workplace have an impact on workers' performance.
- Workers respond to their work environment.
- The existence of informal groups in influencing performance behaviour should not be ignored.
- Style of supervision affected improvement in morale.

Abraham Maslow became associated with a hierarchy of needs and workers' motivation. He put forward the theory that people are motivated to satisfy five basic types of needs. These are:

- Physiological needs: food, water, clothing.
- Safety needs: security and stability.
- Social needs: affection and acceptance by others.
- Esteem needs: feeling of achievement and self-esteem.
- Self-realization need: self-fulfilment.

Motivation to perform depends on the level of needs to be achieved and non-fulfilment of these needs results in dissatisfaction which in turn affects performance.

In spite of lack of evidence and empirical support of the existence of a hierarchy of needs, Maslow's theory became very popular and in fact is still taught in many colleges and universities.

Douglas McGregor: In the early 1960s McGregor put forward a theory relating to the attitude of workers towards work and the style of supervision. If an organization assumes that people do not like to work, do not want responsibility and will avoid it if they can, then there has to be very tight supervision of such workers. Workers' performance would be dependent on the style of supervision. These were the Theory X assumptions.

On the other hand, if workers like to work and take responsibility and they perform better with very little supervision then they should be allowed to work with a minimum of supervision and direction. These were the Theory Y assumptions.

Measuring employees' performance

Frederick Herzberg: In 1959 he interviewed 200 engineers to find out what determined their job satisfaction and job dissatisfaction. He found that job satisfaction was related to workers' achievement, recognition and taking responsibility for their jobs (in other words job satisfaction was related to fulfilling higher-level needs). He called the factors that satisfy higher needs **motivators.**

Job dissatisfaction, on the other hand, was related to job environment (physical working conditions, salary, company policies, supervision etc.). Herzberg called the factors which contributed to job dissatisfaction **hygienic factors**.

Both hygienic factors and motivators were necessary to improve performance. Herzberg put great emphasis on injecting responsibility into planning and giving workers freedom to control their work, and on doing the work in whole rather than in small units. In other words, he advocated 'job enrichment'.

Herzberg's theory became very influential. Many organizations adopted it and saw improvements. However, his critics point out that there is no evidence of the relationship between worker satisfaction and productivity and that his theory was too simplified to deal with complex situations.

Expectancy theories

In the late 1960s and 1970s the focus changed from needs theories to examining how people are motivated and what sustains motivation.

Under the umbrella of expectancy theories some management theorists put forward the view that whether a person is motivated or not depends on his perception of the outcome of his effort. If the outcome meets his need then he will be motivated. There has to be a very high link between effort and performance (high expectancy) for him to be motivated.

If a worker wants to be promoted or to have a high salary increase and he attaches a high value to the outcome and, in addition, he feels that to achieve his goal he has to be a high performer, then he will expect high performance to lead to his goal and is motivated to act accordingly. Motivation, according to expectancy theory, is the result of workers making choices depending on their goals and expectations.

Goal setting

Managing Performance

In the late 1960s various theories were put forward focusing attention on workers' goals which become the main drivers of motivation. Goal setting becomes a stimulus to superior performance. Goal setting could be done at individual or organizational level. If workers have participated in setting their goals, research shows that such practice improves performance.

The situation in the 1980s and 1990s

We have not really moved forward in addressing the issues of motivation, performance and reward. How do we motivate the modern knowledge worker?

Many organizations and many management courses, including those at MBA level, have adopted various theories of motivation developed in the past 70 years.

TIME OUT

What do you think motivates the modern workers?

Name five key factors.

1.

2.

3.

4.

5.

As a line manager, what motivates me to give my best performance depends on:

(a) what I expect from my organization and
(b) what I expect to happen to me (my needs).

I expect the following from my organization:

- Clear vision of where the organization is going
- Clear and well-articulated goals
- Opportunity to contribute
- Honesty and fairness
- Creating a climate for learning
- Fostering mutual responsibility
- Development of staff
- Compassion and support in times of crisis
- Fair reward
- Honest and trustworthy leadership
- No 'fat cats'

What I expect to happen to me:

- To be given a chance to develop new skills and competencies
- To be given a chance to become professionally flexible
- To be given an opportunity to contribute to success
- To be trusted
- To be respected
- To be recognized for the work done
- To be coached
- To be supported if the organization is downsizing

Measuring individual performance: The era of performance appraisals

Employees are one of the key groups of stakeholders involved in any organization. Apart from recognizing their interests and expectations, from the perspective of organizations, it is important to measure their performance to determine their effectiveness in making a contribution towards organizational activities and success.

Key reasons for measuring employees' performance

- It is a means of communicating corporate objectives.
- It is a way of synchronizing departmental or team objectives with strategic objectives.
- Establish congruence between employees' expectations and corporate goals.
- People feel they are valued.
- It is a form of communication. "We will tell you how you are doing."
- It is doing SWOT (strengths, weaknesses, opportunities and threats) for employees.
- It is used as a motivation vehicle.
- It provides assessment of employees' development needs.
- It provides information to update skills.
- In some organizations it is used for salary review or promotion of employees or even transfers of employees.
- It forms a basis for counselling, coaching and mentoring.

TIME OUT

For what reasons are performance appraisals used in your organization?

1.

2.

3.

4.

What is performance appraisal?

For a long time managers or supervisors appraised their subordinates by impressions. There were no set criteria or systematic procedures. In the early 1950s Peter Drucker popularized the notion of 'manager performance and development' and 'management by objectives'. In his book *The Practice of Management*, published in 1955, Drucker wrote:

It is fairly easy to determine what objectives are needed for *manager performance and development*. A business – to stay in business and remain profitable – needs goals in respect to the direction of its managers by objectives and self-control, the setting up of their jobs, the spirit of the management organization, the structure of management and the development of tomorrow's managers. And once the goals are clear, it can always be determined whether they are being attained or not.

He goes on to say:

We are in a bad way, however, when we come to setting objectives for *worker performance and attitude*. It is not that the area is 'intangible'. It is only too tangible; but we know too little about it so far, operate largely by superstitions, omens and slogans rather than by knowledge.

To think through the problems in this area and to arrive at meaningful measurements is one of the great challenges to management.

Management did rise to this challenge and introduced a formalized appraisal system for their employees. However, many managers were uncomfortable in playing God. Douglas McGregor in his book *The Human Side of Enterprise* (1960) wrote:

The conventional approach, unless handled with consummate skill and delicacy, constitutes something close to a violation of the integrity of the personality.

Managers are uncomfortable when they are put in the position of playing God. The respect we hold for the inherent value of the individual leaves us distressed when we must take the responsibility for judging the personal worth of a fellow man.

Yet the conventional approach to performance appraisal forces us, not only to make such judgements and to see them acted upon, but also to communicate them to those we have judged. Small wonder we resist.

Performance appraisals today

Performance appraisal has become the systematic evaluation of employees with respect to their **performance** and their **potential for development**. The operative words are performance, potential and development. Most organizations appraise the performance of their employees.

One of the key aspects of performance appraisal is its link to corporate objectives. Without such a link the appraisal has no meaning and no context. In 1965 the British Institute of Management published a pamphlet, 'Improving Management Performance', which described an integrated approach to business planning and motivation of employees.

However, it has been over 30 years since the publication of this pamphlet and yet one still comes across an appraisal system not linked to corporate objectives.

Methods of appraisal

1 Behaviourally Anchored Rating Scales (BARS)

In the 1960s psychologists developed a method of appraisal known as Behaviourally Anchored Rating Scales (BARS). It focused on behaviour and dimensions of work.

An Example of BARS
Some of the job dimensions of the Head of Department of Marketing.

Understands corporate objectives.	Excellent	Good	Fair	Poor
Knows how to prepares marketing plan.	Excellent	Good	Fair	Poor
Knows how to communicate.	Excellent	Good	Fair	Poor
Knows how to motivate his staff.	Excellent	Good	Fair	Poor
Knows how to conduct meetings.	Excellent	Good	Fair	Poor
Knows how to deal with numbers.	Excellent	Good	Fair	Poor
Knows how to handle computers.	Excellent	Good	Fair	Poor
Knows how to prepare spreadsheets.	Excellent	Good	Fair	Poor
Knows how to write a management report.	Excellent	Good	Fair	Poor
Knows how to prepare budget.	Excellent	Good	Fair	Poor

For each job dimension there are several anchors which are specific statements that show actual job performance. A separate rating form is developed for each job performance.

The observations of behaviour would be expressed in terms of expectations (which could be positive or negative) which are scaled.

Developing BARS

1. There must be active participation of the job holders and their managers or leaders.
2. Identify the key job dimensions.
3. Describe job behaviour by examples (e.g. does it well/ does not do it well) that relate to various degrees of job performance.
4. Rate each item of job behaviour by assigning it a number from 1 (low rating) to 9 (high rating).
5. Compute average scale value for each behaviour.
6. The items of job behaviour with their scores become the anchors for each job dimension.

The BARS method did not gain popularity because many organizations found it time-consuming, costly and complex. There are also problems of establishing ratings.

2 Graphic Rating Scales

Graphic Rating Scales are a popular format for appraising employees. They show the appraisee's relative strengths and weaknesses on specific performance dimensions and on overall performance ratings.

An Example of Graphic Rating Scales (only six dimensions selected)

Employee: **Jack Daniels**
Job: **Training Officer**

	Poor	Fair	Good	Very good	Outstanding	Rating
1 Job Knowledge **Knows how to prepare budgets.**	1	2	3	4	5	4
2 Attitude **Interest in what he does.**	1	2	3	4	5	4
3 Quality of work **Careful and thorough.**	1	2	3	4	5	4
4 Co-operation **Helps when required.**	1	2	3	4	5	3

5 Working in Teams						
Fits in well.	1	2	3	4	5	3

6 Interpersonal skills						
Relates well with others.	1	2	3	4	5	2

SCORING

Total:	20
Outstanding:	25–30
Very good:	20–24
Good:	15–23
Fair:	10–22
Poor:	0–9

Strengths: _____

_____

_____

Weaknesses: _____

_____

_____

Action to be taken: _____

_____

_____

_____

One could also have a graphic picture of the performance of Mr Jack Daniels (Figure 4.1).

Problems with measurements

- There is no scientific way of measuring an employee's rating.
- The rater still has to make a judgement.
- In some cases there is a tendency for a rater to give a middle rate (3 out of 5, for example). Central tendency.
- There is a tendency to stereotype (marking according to our perception of the person in question).

Figure 4.1
Performance profile of
Jack Daniels

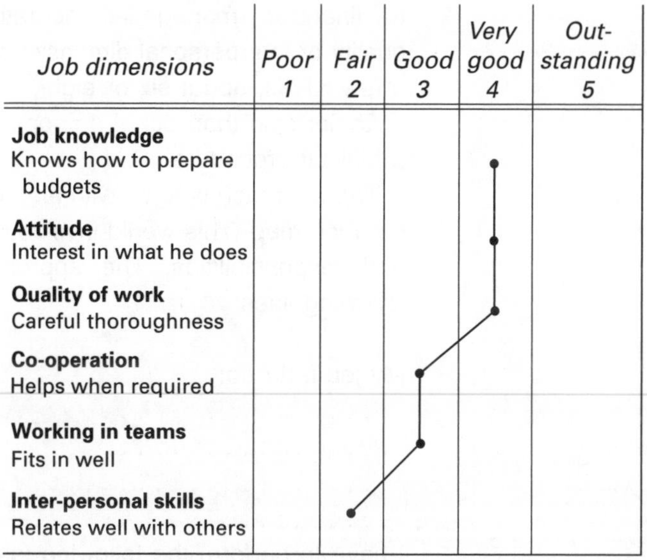

Job dimensions	Poor 1	Fair 2	Good 3	Very good 4	Out-standing 5
Job knowledge Knows how to prepare budgets				●	
Attitude Interest in what he does				●	
Quality of work Careful thoroughness				●	
Co-operation Helps when required			●		
Working in teams Fits in well			●		
Inter-personal skills Relates well with others		●			

■ Rating could be done based on an overall impression of a person – halo effect.

■ Leniency. The rater may feel that a high rating would reflect well on his competence, especially if he is an employee's supervisor.

There are many variations of the system used in practice and all of them have some shortcomings. The main point is that organizations have to appraise their employees and do it properly and meaningfully.

How to design performance appraisals

It is very important that employees should be very actively involved in formulating their own goals. This is an important aspect of motivating employees. It encourages individuals to exert effort.

Ask the staff to think about their job. They are the best people to analyse their jobs; ask them to identify all activities relating to their job.

Categorize all activities under Key Results Areas (KRAs) or Key Performance Areas (KPAs). These KRAs could relate

Managing Performance

to financial, managerial, operational, customer service, quality or interpersonal dimensions. It is helpful to have only a few KRAs, about six or eight.

Easier said than done! as some would put it. But it is not a difficult procedure.

The approach is to sit with an individual staff member and do a job map. This would involve identifying tasks, functions and responsibilities. The approach would be along the following lines:

My job is to do: . . . .
. . . .
. . . .
. . . .
. . . .

I have to perform the following tasks: . . . .
. . . .
. . . .
. . . .
. . . .

These tasks involve the following activities: . . . .
. . . .
. . . .
. . . .
. . . .

My objectives are: . . . .
. . . .
. . . .
. . . .
. . . .

My responsibilities are. . . . .
. . . .
. . . .
. . . .
. . . .

Having received all the information the next step is to align an employee's work objectives to departmental objectives. These objectives should be formulated very clearly and they should be SMART (sensible, measurable, achievable, realistic and time-based) objectives.

There should be complete agreement on these objectives. After the objectives have been finalized a manager should communicate expectations from the department or team point of view. These expectations are the desired outcomes. Finally a time should be set as to when results or outcomes are expected.

In a nutshell, the setting up of an appraisal system involves the following:

- What is expected from an individual
- Why it is expected
- How the outcomes are geared to organizational objectives
- When they should be performed
- How the outcomes are going to be measured
- Who is involved in the measuring process

When the appraisal interview is arranged the manager should do his or her homework by getting full information on the individual concerned. The focus of the interview should be on analysis of performance in order to enable an appraisee to participate in assessment of his or her performance. It is important that 'rapport' should be established between the two parties and communication should be non-threatening in tone, open and honest.

The feedback given should address the following questions on behalf of the appraisee:

- What is expected of me?
- How am I doing?
- Am I on target?
- How can I improve?
- What is my reward?
- Where do I go from here?

Finally the appraisal should be written up, recommending the development action to be taken by whom and when.

The performance appraisal cycle is shown in Figure 4.2. The cycle should be iterative.

There are five categories of problems associated with performance appraisals. These are as follows:

- **The measurement problem**: Some organizations find it very difficult to decide what to appraise due to the lack of understanding of the roles and responsibilities involved or due to the ambiguity of roles involved. In some cases

Managing Performance

Figure 4.2 The performance appraisal cycle

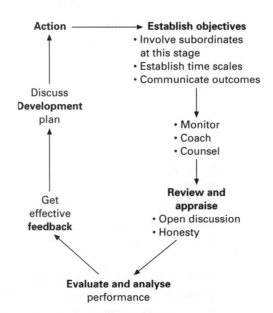

measures formulated are inadequate because not enough thought has gone into designing them.

■ **The judgement problem**: Many managers do not like to act as a judge. There are numerous examples in practice to show disagreements on ratings and interpretations. Such disagreements sour relationships between the parties. Bias also creeps in when judgements are made on behaviour-based indicators.

■ **The organizational problem**: In many companies staff appraisals are not taken seriously. They are used as a window-dressing exercise. Top management get 'we too' feel. Some managers see staff appraisals falling outside their functions and some consider them to be distractions and chores. Appraisals are also cut short because of crises or lack of time.

Many managers also are not trained to conduct appraisals. In one data publication company, 'training' (how you should appraise your staff) is done via e-mails and memos.

■ **The communication problem**: There is lack of communication as to the purpose and the objectives of performance appraisals. For example, in one fast moving consumer goods company one department uses appraisals to determine annual salary increases and profit share whereas the other department uses it to determine the training and development needs of the staff. There is inconsistency between departments and inconsistency between departments and the corporate objectives.

■ **Feedback**: Many managers find in practice that giving honest and constructive feedback to their staff is very uncomfortable and very often they give generalized feedback so as not to offend or annoy the appraisee.

In some training programmes on communication the Johari Window model is used to promote effective communication. This model facilitates communication by using what the parties know of themselves and others (Figure 4.3).

Information about an individual is represented by two perspectives, namely information known and unknown by self and information known and unknown by others. Together they form four categories. They are:

1. **Open category**: information known by both the individual and others.
2. **Blind spot**: Information unknown to the individual but known to others.
3. **Unknown**: Information unknown to both the individual and others.
4. **Facade**: Information known to the individual but not to others.

Figure 4.3 The Johari Window (developed by two psychologists, Joseph Luft and Harry Ingham)

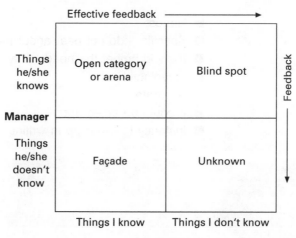

Managing Performance

Figure 4.4 Feedback and Johari Window

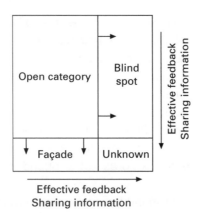

Feedback should affect the shape of the Johari Window. In the appraisal context, if an appraiser is honest and open and willing to share what he or she knows openly then the open category window extends and the shape of the window changes (Figure 4.4). The larger the area of the open category becomes, the more effective feedback becomes.

The other process that affects the shape of the Johari Window is the extent to which the individual is willing to share his or her knowledge and information very openly with others. By doing so the blind spots disappear and again the open category is extended. The sharing of information by self is 'disclosure'. We are referring to disclosure within the work setting.

The success of appraisal, therefore, depends on effective feedback. To be effective feedback should be:

■ Honest
■ Specific – do not beat about the bush
■ It should meet the needs of all parties
■ Meaningful
■ Accurate
■ It could be acted upon
■ Instantly followed up in writing

Measuring employees' performance

Design your own appraisal system (take the initiative for your own performance).

Assessing your performance in 10 steps:

Step 1. Write down the main objectives of your organization.
Step 2. Write down the main objectives of your department or section or team.
Step 3. Are these objectives consistent? If not, or if you are not sure, discuss with your supervisor or manager or team leader.
Step 4. What is your job?
Step 5. What are the Key Results Areas of your job? Identify critical elements. Consider their impact on results and their impact on others.
Step 6. Discuss your KRAs with your supervisor or manager.
Step 7. What are the activities involved in relation to your KRAs?
Step 8. Think about how you want these activities measured.
Step 9. Prepare the rating scale and discuss this scale with your supervisor or manager.
Step 10. Try appraising yourself first before the formal appraisal in order to get the feel of the measurement.

What are the advantages of asking an employee to design his or her own system?

1. It overcomes resistance.
2. An employee is actively involved.
3. The employee knows his or her job better than anyone in the organization.
4. There will be an element of trust and honesty.
5. The employee's supervisor or manager acts as a coach, facilitator and mentor.
6. Creates ownership.
7. Training and development needs are properly identified.
8. Effective communication takes place.
9. An employee's work becomes meaningful.
10. Self-assessment becomes consistent with empowerment.

Performance and the reward system

Performance appraisals in my view should be used to continually assess and improve the performance of an individual. In other words, it should be used for development purposes. However, some organizations link performance appraisals to reward. If this is the case it should be made very clear how it works.

In 1977 Edward Lawler put forward the following five factors that should be considered in designing a reward system:

1. Satisfaction depends on the amount received and the amount the individual feels he should receive.
2. Comparison with what happens to others influences people's feelings of satisfaction.
3. An employee's satisfaction with both intrinsic and extrinsic rewards received affects overall job satisfaction.
4. Different people desire different rewards and they attach different values to rewards.
5. Many rewards satisfy only because they lead to other rewards (more leisure time, for example).

The reward system, therefore, should have the following attributes:

- Equity
- Fairness
- Effectiveness
- Motivator
- Satisfy needs
- Linked to performance

360-degree appraisals and feedback method

102

Many organizations now are experimenting with the 360-degree appraisal system. Essentially this method is based on receiving feedback from colleagues, managers, supervisors, team leaders, suppliers and customers. In other words, all the groups of people (stakeholders) with whom the

Figure 4.5 360-degree
feedback system

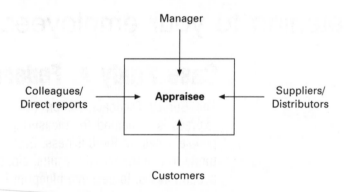

individual comes in close contact in performing his or her
task. See Figure 4.5.

The information is collected through questionnaires and
the feedback is given anonymously. The team leader or a
manager then sits with the individual to analyse the
feedback.

Advantages of this method

- The feedback is comprehensive.
- It enables the individual to assess the impact he or she
  makes on the people he or she is dealing with.
- It gives the individual an opportunity to benchmark his or
  her perception against that of others.
- It is balanced feedback in that all stakeholders are
  considered.
- It appears fair.
- It reflects behaviour rather than judgement.
- It is meaningful.

Which organizations are using it?

Here are some examples:

Levi Strauss North America
Johnson & Johnson
Federal Express
Motorola
General Electric
W. H. Smith
Tesco

Listening to your employees

Case Study A: Federal Express

The Survey Feedback Action (SFA) Programme at Federal Express is a method for measuring and then improving the people aspect of the business. Each manager has the opportunity to use the survey results, along with the feedback and action phases, to design a blueprint for improving workgroup satisfaction and effectiveness.

According to the information given by Kevin Dunkeld, Manager – Personnel Services, the SFA "surveys all employees on a voluntary basis each year to identify areas of strengths and weaknesses. The survey ensures that upper management is aware of employee concerns, and it provides a vehicle for continuous improvement."

There are three phases of the SFA programme They are:

Survey: Employees are asked to complete a survey which has questions concerning management, the work environment, programmes and policies. The survey is designed to be completed in an environment that enables employees to feel free to give honest feedback. An employee's responses are confidential so that no one can find out how an individual responded.

Feedback: When managers receive results of the survey for the work group, they schedule a series of feedback meetings during which they discuss concerns with the employees and develop action plans to facilitate improvements.

Action: After conducting the initial feedback sessions, all managers must complete a Quality Action Plan which they will need to introduce and monitor in the months ahead.

FedEx produce guidelines for leaders on how to interpret reports, how to analyse reports for discussion, how to plan for feedback meetings, writing the Quality Action Plan and using the Quality Action Plan for improving results. The SFA is used as a means, not an end. "Its ultimate aim is continuous improvement in the workplace through better employee involvement and communication."

Case Study B: Staff performance management at W. H. Smith

John Ainley, Group Human Resources Director at W. H. Smith Group plc, has been very kind in supplying me with information on 'Using feedback in the Performance Management Process'.

Bill Cockburn, the chief executive of W. H. Smith, joined on 1 January1996. Upon his appointment he instituted a major change initiative. Today W.H. Smith Group consists of five businesses: WHS Retail, Waterstones, Virgin/Our Price, News and USA. The group employs 32 000 people and each business is led by its own board.

The group focuses its attention on people leadership, customers and resource allocations. In 1989 employee research was carried out to find out what employees wanted from work and what would enable them to give their best to customers. The following issues emerged from the survey:

■ Employees wanted to be free from unnecessary rules,
■ they wanted responsibility,
■j they wanted to be valued,
■ they wanted to have a say in what is going on, and
■ they wanted to be told what is going on.

What they were after was respect, empowerment and open communication.

How the staff felt about the company and management affected the delivery of service excellence. A retailing organization is transparent to its customers – customers walk among the employees.

W. H. Smith decided to challenge the 'status quo' and introduced upward appraisal. How was it done?

1. They put together attributes of what staff considered a good manager to be.
2. They came up with a list of 32 attributes.
3. Staff were asked to score their managers on a 1 to 5 scale against those attributes.
4. Staff were asked to rank their top six most important attributes.
5. Staff were asked to categorize themselves by age, gender, and the nature of their reporting relationship with their manager.

The staff are asked to complete and return the form anonymously to a third-party data processing agency. The agency process the data and the results are sent to the manager who is being assessed. The results are compared to a divisional average. The manager then has the opportunity to discuss the results with his or her own manager. After initial resistance the scheme came to be part of the way W. H. Smith do their business.

Based on the success of upward appraisal (the process has never been labelled 'Upward Appraisal' internally – it has always been known as a 'Management Style' survey), the group introduced a 360-degree appraisal system. This involved feedback from staff, self, peers, internal customers and the manager.

In the first trial the staff were asked to comment upon performance in two respects:

■ Achievement of performance objectives, and
■ Development against their competencies

The competencies highlighted were:

Initiative and achievement	Gathering information
Customer focus	Critical reasoning
Adaptable and flexible	Strategic perspective
Personal strength	Task management
Awareness of others	Influencing others
Involving and supporting others	

The jury is still out as far as this system is concerned.

How to succeed in implementing 360-degree feedback

■ The system must be thought out very carefully before it is implemented.
■ All employees must be informed of how this system works and the reasons for introducing it.
■ Do not introduce it as a window-dressing exercise. Avoid the 'me too' syndrome.
■ Those conducting appraisals need to be trained properly.
■ There has to be a culture of trust in the organization.

- The system should focus not only on tasks but also on relationships.
- There should be a consensus on core values and alignment of individual and corporate values.
- The action plan should focus on improvements and enhancement of core competencies.

A 360-degree appraisal process and research results

The following section is taken from an article, 'Designing an Effective 360-Degree Appraisal Feedback Process', by David Antonioni. It appeared in *Organizational Dynamics*, Autumn 1996 issue.

The model shown (Figure 4.6) provides one way of considering the components of a 360-degree system and their impact on possible outcomes. The model is based, in large part, on research results from a 360-degree research program conducted through the University of Wisconsin-Madison. Thus far, four midsize companies (two manufacturing and two service) have participated in the research program. Three of the companies have included many but not all of the components presented in the model, and one company has followed the model completely.

Research was conducted using focus group, survey studies, and follow-up interviews in all four of the organizations. Experimental studies were conducted within two of the organizations. Figure 4.7 summarizes some of the findings from the surveys and experimental studies.

The model attempts to both describe the entire system – considered as consisting of inputs, processes, and outcomes – and specify the components within the system. The model proposes that quality inputs, when processed effectively, will lead to desired outcomes. This means that organizations must provide organizational support to the inputs and processes component of the 360-degree system in order to attain desired outcomes.

Our research ... underscore an important point. Organizations considering implementing 360-degree appraisals would do well to first define specific desired outcomes and then to develop specific processes to attain those outcomes. Some visionary outcomes, such as reduction of undiscussables, voluntarily informal

Managing Performance

Input	Process	Output
1. Purpose of appraisal: developmental vs. evaluating	1. Self-appraisal	1. Increase awareness of others' expectations
	2. Reaction to feedback	
	3. Coaching steps	
2. The appraisal form	4. Targeting improvement	2. Improvements in appraisee work behaviour/performance
3. Written feedback		
4. Appraiser anonymity	5. Action plans	
5. Selecting per appraisers	6. Reporting results back to appraisers	
		3. Reduction of undiscussables
6. Appraiser training	7. Specific goals/action	
7. Training for appraisees	8. Just-in-time training	4. Increase in periodic informal 360-degree performance reviews
	9. Mini assessment/follow-up	
8. Training for coaches		
9. Feedback report	10. Recognition for improvements	5. Management training
	11. Accountability	

Figure 4.6 A 360-degree appraisal process: a practitioner's model

performance reviews, and management learning, will stretch organizational members in a constructive way. These outcomes may give 360-degree appraisals a meaningful purpose that goes beyond being just another appraisal.

A summary of 360-degree research results

1. Appraisers prefer that 360-degree appraisals be used for developmental feedback, not to make decisions about an appraisee's merit raises – appraisers are concerned about negative reactions from the appraisees.
2. Appraisees feel that written descriptive 360-degree feedback is more helpful than rating scale data.
3. Managers want their direct contributors to be accountable for their rating, however, direct contributors want the ratings to remain anonymous.
4. Direct contributors who had to sign their names to the upward appraisal instruments gave their managers higher ratings than those who used an anonymous procedure.
5. Managers indicated that about 25 per cent of the appraisal feedback they received was expected positive feedback, 30 per cent unexpected positive feedback, 20 to 30 per cent expected negative feedback, and 15 to 20 per cent unexpected negative feedback.

6. Appraisers (direct contributors) estimated that 19 per cent of the managers would be surprised by the low ratings on the 360-degree appraisals.
7. Only 50 per cent of appraisers reported that managers had shared summary results of their upward appraisals.
8. Appraisees who score high on achievement motivation and who perceive high value to the appraisal feedback are more likely to discuss their appraisal results with the appraisers.
9. Appraisees tend not to develop specific goals and action plan based on the 360-degree feedback.
10. Appraisees were often left to figure out for themselves how to improve low-rated supervisory behaviours.
11. Seventy-two per cent of the appraisees reported that their immediate supervisors had not followed up on action plans based on the 360-degree appraisal results.
12. Eighty-seven per cent of the appraisees felt appraisers had not recognized their efforts to improve their work behaviours.

(Source: Antonioni, D. (1996). Designing an Effective 360-Degree Appraisal Feedback Process. *Organizational Dynamics*, Autumn. Reprinted by permission of the publisher © 1996 American Management Association, New York. All rights reserved.)

Going through corporate rituals

Finally, the following conversations were heard 'a night before and the morning after' performance appraisal:

Executive A: "I have an appraisal with my boss tomorrow. I am dreading it! I have not been able to sleep for days now."
Executive B: "Why are you so nervous about appraisal? You should look forward to it. After all the main purpose is to find out whether you are doing OK work or not."
Executive A: "You are joking. You do not know my team leader. He goes through every item on the appraisal form like a tooth comb. He tries to find as many faults as he can and the whole atmosphere becomes threatening. I get the impression if he can find numerous faults his boss thinks he is doing a good job and his next promotion and pay rise depends on how hard he is with his staff."

Managing Performance

Executive B: "I must admit I do not look forward to my appraisal. It is not threatening but we seem to be going over the same points every time we have appraisals. You never know what his plan is. We are asked to prepare negative and positive points about our work and when we meet I mention these points and he writes them down. He does not come up with any list of negative and positive points himself.

"We do discuss these points and he promises to arrange training programmes if I ask him but these programmes never materialize. He always says there is no budget for it so now I do not bother."

Executive A: "A day after appraisal (morning after) he distances himself from me and I myself feel very uncomfortable. I wait every day to receive some sort of warning in writing but it does not happen. Maybe one of these days the list of my negatives is going to get so long that I will be asked to leave."

Executive B: "My supervisor feels relieved after appraisal. He tells me that he finds appraisal interviews time-consuming and that they take him away from his real work."

Write down your thoughts on the conversation between Executive A and Executive B.

TIME OUT

_____

_____

_____

_____

_____

_____

_____

_____

_____

How do we feel about our appraisals?

The Institute of Personnel and Development (IPD) conducted a survey on performance appraisals and published its findings in March 1996. Briefly they were:

■ Sixty per cent of those surveyed felt motivated by appraisals.
■ Eleven per cent felt demotivated.
■ Seventy-seven per cent felt they could talk openly at appraisals.
■ Almost a third felt their boss considered appraisals to be a bureaucratic chore.
■ Sixty-five per cent said appraisals are used to identify training and developmental needs.
■ Forty-six per cent thought it was fair to use appraisals to determine pay rises.
■ Forty-seven per cent of managers who conduct appraisals said employees use the occasion to moan.
■ Fifteen per cent of managers who carried out appraisals did not like doing so.
■ Almost a third agreed that your appraisal rating depends on whether your boss likes you.
■ Overall most appraisals have a positive effect on employees.

Done honestly and properly employees should look forward to their appraisals. It is an occasion to review their capabilities and performance and develop plans to update skills and gain new competencies to remain employable.

Selected reading

Antonioni D. (1966) Designing an Effective 360-degree Appraisal Feedback Process. *Organizational Dynamics*, Autumn.
Armstrong M. (1970). *A Handbook of Personnel Management Practice*. Kogan Page.
Drucker P. (1950) *The Practice of Management*. Butterworth-Heinemann.
Drucker P. (1964). *Managing For Results*. Butterworth-Heinemann.
Drucker P. (1967). *The Effective Executive*. Butterworth-Heinemann.
Gordon R. J. (1987). *Organizational Behaviour*. Allyn and Bacon Inc.
O'Reilly, B. (1994). 360-degree feedback can change your life. *Fortune*, 17 October.
People Management. March 1996 issue.

5

Performing for your customers

You don't lose weight by buying a better scale.
Philip Crosby

■ Winning performance and business success are matters of delivering service excellence. What matters these days is not just what is produced (product quality) but how it is delivered (service quality).

■ Peter Drucker has been writing about caring for customers for over 40 years. Other management 'gurus' including Tom Peters and Rosabeth Moss Kanter have consistently been preaching about establishing strategic partnerships with customers.

■ Total quality initiatives in the 1980s focused on transforming the complete organization into a quality culture. Various award schemes have been initiated in the USA and Europe to encourage total quality initiatives.

■ The focus of attention in the 1990s shifted to getting close to customers. Organizations deploy various avenues towards getting close to customers.

■ These include questionnaires, visiting customers, providing 0800 numbers, forming customer focus groups, mystery shopping and various surveys.

Performing for your customers

■ What do executives think of customer service now and in the next five years? A Survey on Service by Digital Equipment Co.
■ It is important to integrate quality, employee satisfaction and customer satisfaction to improve business performance.
■ Customer satisfaction – Sun Microsystems' way: A case study.
■ Customer satisfaction: Key success factors.

Winning performance is a matter of meeting your customers' needs and perceptions. In the 1990s many organizations, both profit and not-for-profit, have come to realize that what matters most is not what you deliver but how you deliver it.

For a very long time the focus on customer satisfaction revolved around product warranties and the products themselves. I recall a statement made by one senior vice president of a company manufacturing washing machines. He said, "We make the best washing machines. I simply cannot understand why customers do not buy them." This was the thinking that prevailed throughout the nineteenth century.

Management 'gurus' on customers

Peter Drucker

Drucker has been writing about customers for a number of years. Following are extracts from his various writings:

> If you want to know what a business is we have to start with its purpose . . . There is only one valid definition of business: to create a customer.
>
> *The Practice of Management* (1955)

> What the people in the business think they know about customer and market is more likely to be wrong than right. There is only one person who really knows: customer. Only by asking the customer, by watching him, by trying to understand his behaviour can one find out who he is, what he does, how he buys, how he uses what he buys, what he expects, what he values, and so on.
>
> *Managing For Results* (1964), p. 87

Managing Performance

Specifically, there are no results within the organizations. All the results are outside. The only business results, for instance, are produced by a customer who converts the costs and efforts of the business into revenues and profits through his willingness to exchange his purchasing power for the products or services for the business.

The Effective Executive (1966), p.11

The customer never buys a product. By definition the customer buys the satisfaction of a want. The customer buys value. Yet the manufacturer, by definition, cannot produce a value, but can only make and sell a product . . .

Tasks, Responsibilities, Practices: Management (1974), p.76

Tom Peters

In the book *In Search of Excellence* (1982) (co-authored with Robert Waterman), they devote a whole chapter on staying close to the customer.

Staying close to the customer, they emphasized, was one of the key business imperatives. Many companies pay lip service to customer service; customers are considered a nuisance. In highlighting the success of 'excellent' companies they write, "the excellent companies really are close to their customers." They have an obsession with customers, service, quality and listening to their customers.

In all his books and seminars delivered in the past 15 years Peters has emphasized the importance of staying close to the customers. He has advocated extending the customer satisfaction goal to delighting the customers. All his books and seminars are peppered with successful companies delighting their customers.

Rosabeth Moss Kanter

In her book *When Giants Learn to Dance* (1989), Kanter writes about the customers' role in helping business achieve its goals. She wrote about forming alliances with customers and other stakeholders. Good customer relationships sharpen the effectiveness of the organization.

- Customer relationships are important because:
  - they are the single best source of new business,
  - by listening to them products and production can be aligned to their requirements,
  - they can also become a source of ideas and innovation.

Performance based on total quality

During the 1980s many organizations adopted total quality initiatives in order to improve their performance. The journey to quality was initiated by companies like Motorola, Miliken and ICL.

The following quality 'gurus' made a significant impact on many blue chip organizations.

Joseph M. Juran

Juran has remained a leading proponent of quality for more than 50 years. He has written several seminal books on quality. His significant contribution was his formulation of methods of creating a customer-oriented organization. Achieving quality, he emphasized throughout his career, is about communication, management commitment and people.

He advocated systematic adoption of a total quality initiative. Organizations should build awareness of the need for quality and organize and set realistic goals to achieve their quality objectives. They should invest in training their staff and recognize them for their achievements. There is also a need to measure and monitor progress continuously.

W. Edwards Deming

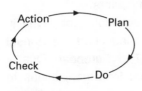

Figure 5.1
The Deming cycle

Deming is considered by many to be the father of the Japanese quality movement. He advocated that managers play a leading role in driving the improvement in quality. Quality, according to Deming, should be planned, implemented, and monitored continuously. He developed a very simple method of problem solving which is now popularly known as the Deming cycle (Figure 5.1).

He also emphasized the importance of changing the attitude towards quality, training staff, creating a climate of trust and driving out fear, breaking inter-departmental barriers, and using tools and techniques of quality.

Philip B. Crosby

Crosby was associated with the 'zero defects' movement in the 1960s. He advocated top management commitment to quality, formation of quality improvement teams, encouraging individuals to establish improvement goals, recognizing staff achievements in relation to quality standards, and treating quality as a journey rather than a destination.

Quality performance awards

Besides these 'gurus' various award schemes were instituted in the 1980s to promote quality awareness and performance in the USA and Europe. In the USA, the Baldrige Award was instituted in 1987. Each year two awards are given in each of the two categories, namely, manufacturing and service and small business.

The areas of performance on which assessment is made are leadership, information and analysis, strategy quality planning, human resource utilization, quality assurance of products and services, quality results and customer satisfaction. The last area (customer satisfaction) is weighted more heavily than any other area.

As far as the customer satisfaction component is concerned, examiners are looking for the way organizations determine customer requirements and expectations; customer relationship management; customer service standards; commitment to customers; complaint resolution for quality improvement; customer satisfaction comparison, which involves comparisons with competitors.

In Europe, the European Foundation for Quality Management was set up in 1988. It launched the annual European Quality Award in 1992. The European Quality Model, which provides the framework for organizations to assess their performance as quality organizations, is divided into 'enablers' and 'results'. The 'enablers' are leadership, people management, policy and strategy, resources and processes. The 'results' are people satisfaction, customer satisfaction, impact on society and business results.

The quality initiative was to become the main driver towards business performance and towards achieving competitive edge in a fast-changing competitive climate.

Parallel to the movement towards quality, some organizations started restructuring their organizations towards delivering service excellence. Customer service became the slogan and the focus for many organizations. According to Tom Peters, the organizational challenge "is to view every element of every operation through the customer's lens; to constantly attempt to – literally – redefine each element of the business in terms of the customer's perceptions of the intangibles".

For a number of years, in marketing terms the focus was on competing on the four Ps (Product, Place, Promotion and Price). Every marketing student and every marketing textbook up to now emphasizes competing on these four Ps. However, in the 1990s the focus shifted to competing on customer service and customer retention.

Quality has two dimensions: product quality (what is produced) and service quality (how it is delivered). This chapter is based on achieving business success by providing service quality.

Harvard Business Review articles on customers

(1) March–April 1955. B. Joseph Pine II, Don Peppers and Martha Rogers ask 'Do You Want to Keep Your Customers FOREVER?' They argue that many businesses do not use the available technology to give their customers what they want, when they want it, where they want it and how they want it. To keep their customers, companies must use technology to become a *mass customizer* and *one-to-one marketer*. Focusing on these two dimensions will bind producers and customers in a *learning relationship*.

In learning relationships, individual customers teach the company more and more about their preferences and needs, giving the company immense competitive advantage. The more customers teach the company, the better it becomes at providing exactly what they want – exactly how they want it – and the more difficult it will be for a competitor to entice them away.

A company's *customer share* – its share of each customer's total patronage – is one of the most useful measures of success in building a learning relationship. To calculate customer share a company must have some idea of what the customer is buying from the competition and what he or she might be willing to buy from the company. The best source of such information is the customer.

Yet another important performance measure is what we call *customer sacrifice*: the gap between what each customer truly wants and needs and what the company can supply. To understand individual customer sacrifice, companies building learning relationships must go beyond the aggregate customer-satisfaction figures that almost everyone collects today.

They give various examples of companies who have done just that.

(2) May–June, 1995. Louise O'Brien and Charles Jones ask 'Do Rewards Really Create Loyalty?' Rewards are important but they argue too many organizations use rewards as short-term promotional give-aways or specials of the month. Companies need to think about the ways and the systems through which customers are continually educated about the rewards of loyalty and motivated to earn them.

The full potential of value sharing through rewards is realized only when customers change their habits to become sustainably loyal. And that shift occurs only when the company has developed and communicated a proposition that clearly has long-term benefits for the customer.

Many of the rewards and loyalty programs in the marketplace today reveal a limited understanding of customer needs and desires. From a customer's perspective five elements determine a program's value. They are cash value, choice of redemption options, aspirational value, relevance and convenience. Few programs today offer all five, but companies that want to play the rewards game should be sure their value measures up to customers' alternatives.

How do businesses listen to customers?

Before we look at this aspect consider the following.

How does your organization listen
to customers?

TIME OUT

_____

_____

_____

_____

_____

_____

_____

_____

_____

Questionnaires

Questionnaires are left in hotel bedrooms, on planes, and most of them are sent by post to enable customers to give their feedback. Some organizations undertake telephone surveys to find out if their customers are satisfied with the products they purchased and the service they received.

Some organizations gather all the feedback but they do not analyse the feedback to take appropriate action because of lack of resource, lack of time or simply lacking the knowledge to interpret the feedback or not having the system to handle responses. However, they take comfort in knowing that they are in touch with their customers!

Customer focus group

Customers are invited by the organizations to give their views on products and services. The format varies according to the agenda set by the organizations. Some invite customers to discuss a specific topic such as on-time delivery or product design.

Managing Performance

Such a system is time-consuming, expensive and in some cases difficult to facilitate. There is also a problem of deciding who to invite. It is very important to get customers who have not been satisfied with your products or service.

Help line

Many organizations, especially computer companies, now have help lines. If you are having any problem you can get in touch with the help desk to attend to your problems.

In some cases not enough thinking or resources have gone into considering the function of the help line. The author knows of one popular computer company which changed the location of the help desk from England to Ireland. It took a particular customer three and a half months to get through and incurred considerable telephone cost. (Every time this particular customer phoned there was music and then a voice to say someone will attend you as you are in the queue. In fact the message kept repeating itself and there was no person at the other end. This he found out after writing to the company. The company refused to reimburse the cost.)

Visits to customers

Some companies send their staff to visit customers. These visits are made with sales people or sometimes by senior managers.

Customers' councils

Some organizations have instituted customers' councils. Theses are groups of customers who meet regularly to advise the company. In some organizations they are called advisory committees.

Customer research

Research is undertaken either by outside bodies or by organizations themselves to find out what their customers think of their product or service. Again one has to be very careful in setting questions and interpreting feedback.

0800 numbers

It is now very popular for organizations to encourage their customers to phone them by going for 0800 numbers which are non-chargeable.

Mystery shoppers

In some organizations certain staff from the same organization act as shoppers and customers to get first-hand experience of the service provided by their organization. They then make a report to highlight good points as well as deficiencies. They also visit their competitors to benchmark against their competitors' standard of service.

The American Customer Satisfaction Index

The Index is a joint project of the University of Michigan Business School and the American Society for Quality Control. It is based on a random sample of the actual users of 3900 products and services. The companies were selected on the basis of their size and US market share. According to *Fortune*, roughly 30 000 people participated in the telephone surveys in each of two years. For detailed results covering various sectors see *Fortune*, 11 December 1995, p. 96.

Swedish Customer Satisfaction Barometer

Professor Claes Fornell, who is the founder of the American Customer Satisfaction Index, also founded the Swedish Customer Satisfaction Barometer in 1989.

Information is gathered by telephone interviews with 35 000 customers of private and public organizations. The interviews try to measure customer perceptions of service, quality and meeting customer expectations. Various factors are weighted to give an overall customer satisfaction measurement.

European-wide customer satisfaction measurement

In Germany Das Deutsche Kundenbarometer was established in 1992 and similar indices are being developed in France, Italy and Denmark.

In the European Union the European Commission's Directorate-General III is involved in developing a European index on competitiveness which will lead to companies throughout the Union paying more attention to quality and delivering service excellence.

Getting close to customers: Survey results

In 1992 Digital Equipment Company in association with John Humble and Management Centre Europe undertook a survey of executive opinion. According to the following results, organizations are trying to get close to their customers:

Measuring customer satisfaction: Effective methods

	Europe %	USA %	Japan %	UK %
Personal visits by management	87	89	99	91
Personal visits by sales people	88	85	99	88
Analysis of complaints received	87	90	98	86
Questionnaires	65	97	98	68
Independent observation & assessments	65	52	99	64
Focus meeting with groups of customers	71	60	99	62
Toll-free phones	39	51	99	27

(Source: Service – a Survey of UK Executive Opinion. Digital Equipment Co.)

Some examples of companies that adopt different methods

In **Whirlpool Europe** there is a systematic feedback process. Employees take very a active part in making suggestions as to how to improve customer service. There is a customer advocate forum where employees act as advocates on behalf of their customers to resolve customers' issues brought to their attention.

Avon Products Inc. use a service quality survey method called 'serqual' to measure the customer's expectation and perceptions. Through this method they found out that their customers wanted 0800 telephone service, personal service relationships and easier ordering methods.

In **Canon Europa N.V.** they focused their attention on the following in order to facilitate improvement in customer satisfaction:

- problem escalation of service calls,
- problems fixed on first visit,
- spare part availability,
- personnel available to solve problems,
- response times, and
- communication regarding the results of service calls.

At **Kwik-Fit** they make over 200 000 calls per month contacting over 100 000 customers within 72 hours of their visit to a Kwik-Fit centre. Eighty-five per cent of those contacted are willing to co-operate and take part in surveys.

At **DHL** they have a 'cradle to grave' philosophy of managing customers. 'Cradle to grave' is an approach to communication planning which is responsive to the current requirements and potential of a customer as their relationship with a supplier grows. As in any relationship there are various different phases. What 'cradle to grave' enables one to do is to establish exactly where in the customer life cycle you are currently sitting and to tailor your communication precisely to address that position. For example, at the beginning of a new business relationship one is not encouraged to talk about the benefits of long-term strategic partnerships. At an early stage it is important to introduce customers to a range of services offered to meet their needs.

Managing Performance

American Airlines are now installing 'power to the seat' to enable business travellers to use their laptop computers. This facility will be available to first class and business class travellers on selected international flights.

Rolls-Royce have decided to align their product range with the aspirations of existing and potential customers, widen and enhance the choice of specifications available and develop the performance characteristics of particular models. They are doing these things to demonstrate that the company listens to its customers.

At **Marks & Spencer** great emphasis is placed on training and developing their front-line staff to have the right attitude and behaviour to deliver good customer service – service that customers can appreciate. They also source their products with the aim of providing their customers with high quality and innovative products.

Dell Computer Corporation undertook a customer survey and found that customers were finding the organization more difficult to do business with because of their administrative infrastructure. They re-engineered their customer interface by using technology effectively and it thus became easy to do business with Dell customers.

Case Study A: Customer service at Avis Europe

Lesley Colyer, Vice President – Personnel, is very proud of the way Avis is catering for its customers and employees. Employee satisfaction and customer satisfaction go hand in hand, according to Ms Colyer.

I am grateful to her for supplying me with the following information on Avis Europe.

"Avis Europe was created in 1965 to spearhead international expansion for its then American parent. Avis came to Europe with a singular vision of 'building the best and fastest growing company with the highest profit margins in the business of renting cars without drivers'. The company went from green-field start to market leader in just eight years. It has remained there ever since. The company's organization structure and management philosophy is one of centralized management and a high degree of local autonomy, underpinned by strong support services at the centre.

Performing for your customers

"Today, the company operates 102 000 vehicles throughout more than 2800 outlets in 96 territories throughout Europe, Africa, and the Middle East. Its vision, like its culture, has not changed in more than three decades. This has resulted in a consistent approach to keeping the business strong . . . continuous investment in three critical areas – its people, its network and its technology. The company's service strategy revolves around customer retention through employee empowerment and a minimum of organizational levels . . . maximum of six between the chairman and those who wash the cars.

"The company firmly believes that continuous improvement of itself will not increase shareholder value or long-term profitability, unless it is focused on what matters most to the customer."

Customer satisfaction measurement

"A company cannot know what matters most to its customers, unless it asks them. In 1989, Avis took a quantum leap forward in the way it listened to customers, by leveraging its technological advantage. Its Wizard system captures virtually every single customer transaction and obtains a wealth of data that is linked to customer and employee opinion and used to drive improvements in areas that most affect customer satisfaction and loyalty.

"From extensive research conducted across 11 countries and involving thousands of customers and all the company's employees, Avis developed satisfaction measurement systems to harmonize with the customer transaction data collected through its Wizard system.

"Every month, over 13 500 customers in 14 countries are contacted and asked to record the level of satisfaction they have experienced with the company's service, product and people for a particular rental and how likely they are to use Avis again as a result of that experience. There are two important points here: First, the service attributes measured are those that have the greatest impact on customer satisfaction and retention in our particular operating environment, as identified in the baseline research. Second, ALL of the attributes measured can be directly influenced and affected by employees at rental counters throughout the Avis system (Figure 5.2).

"From the responses received, with an average about 30 per cent across Europe, comprehensive information is produced and filtered from senior management at Group HQ to every location

Managing Performance

Figure 5.2 Avis satisfaction measurement

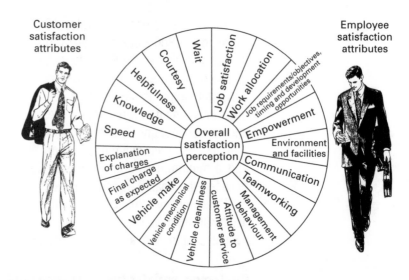

Avis satisfaction measurement

in the network. Each location receives regular and recent feedback from their customers – not just a set of average numbers but individual customer scores, together with the customer transaction number. Local teams are, therefore, not only able to look at the survey results but also to view the full details of the particular transaction on their computer screen. This is very powerful because it helps each team to identify what likely actions, behaviours or circumstances were responsible for the specific customer feedback. Continuous improvement is thus driven at local level by those who deliver the service and is in absolute response to their customers' feedback.

"Continuous improvement in customer satisfaction performance is encouraged through the company's Spirit of Avis recognition programme, which provides individual and team recognition to employees who have 'given a little extra' and made exceptional service the norm rather than the exception.

"But customer feedback is not just used by the company's operational staff. It is used by every discipline to drive improvements that MATTER to the customer.

"The marketing functions are able to track satisfaction by product, by day of the week, by location and by nationality, enabling improvements in product design and development. Additionally, the system provides a wealth of competitive information, used to benchmark service levels and product differentiation.

"The fleet functions are able to track satisfaction by make, model and even colour! As the company is the largest purchaser of fleet in western Europe, this is of significant importance not only to the company, a factor in fleet purchase decisions, but also to the vehicle manufacturers in terms of their fleet design and model acceptability.

"The training and customer service functions are able to identify where changes are needed to processes and procedures; what are the root causes of customer dissatisfaction; what new knowledge and skills need to be emphasized.

"In addition, the data is used externally in a number of ways. This includes evaluation and improvement of partnership products such as frequent flyer programmes and customer satisfaction reports for major customers regarding the satisfaction of their travelling employees. This process forms a key part of contract negotiation and acts as a powerful tool to demonstrate service standards are being achieved and to agree service guarantees.

"The company strongly believes that a truly effective quality and performance process is not just an internal activity. Its ultimate success depends on the extent to which it recognizes and integrates the interests and needs of customers, suppliers and partners alike."

Avis link customer satisfaction with employee satisfaction. According to Ms Colyer the quality of business performance is a direct reflection of the quality of its people. As with customers, the company measures overall satisfaction perception plus levels of satisfaction on a number of employment attributes that directly affect customer satisfaction and retention.

Employee satisfaction measurement

"The employee satisfaction survey is sent annually to all employees and follows the same results cascade process as the customer surveys, i.e. from senior management through to specific areas of the business. Responses to the surveys are typically between 70 and 80 per cent. At a corporate level, the results are used to identify areas for improvement and company-wide initiatives are introduced in response. But as with the customer data, continuous improvement is driven at local level through locally developed initiatives.

"As an example of the close correlation between customer and employee satisfaction, Figure 5.3 shows the cumulative increases in employee satisfaction in Avis, Spain, across a two-year period. Positive increases were experienced on every

Managing Performance

Figure 5.3 Employee satisfaction survey, Spain (% change FY96 vs. FY 94)

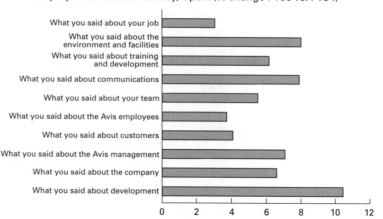

Employee satisfaction survey, Spain (% change FY96 vs. FY94)

employment attribute measured. It is no coincidence that over the same time frame, overall customer satisfaction in Spain also increased with satisfaction levels rising in five of the service attributes measured. During the same period, the Spanish company grew its customer base by 45 per cent.

"In the spirit of continuous improvement, both the customer and employee satisfaction survey processes have recently been significantly enhanced. With effect from 1997, the company will integrate the results from both survey sources to provide a holistic tool with which to drive performance improvement."

Sun Microsystems adopted a holistic diagnostic tool in order to drive performance. Below is information on how Sun Microsystems does it.

Case Study B: Customer service at Sun Microsystems

Mike Roberts, a manager involved in Customer Project Office at Sun Microsystems, is very enthusiastic and becomes excited when you ask him about the Sun Quality Index.

Sun Microsystems Inc. is one of America's fastest growing companies, with a turnover of nearly $46 billion. It is one of the leading providers of UNIX workstations, servers and related technologies. It is composed of five operating companies and is located in more than 30 countries world-wide.

Performing for your customers

In 1994 the company introduced the Sun Quality Index (SQI). This Index system consisted of the Customer Quality Index (CQI), the Employee Quality Index (EQI) and the Customer Satisfaction Index (CSI). Since its introduction the Index has been credited with bringing quality focus and direction to Sun employees and decreasing customer dissatisfiers such as late deliveries and defective products.

How do these indices work?

Customer Quality Index

This index is composed of the weighted sum of 33 'customer verified' sources of dissatisfaction. These dissatisfiers are weighted according to their relative importance to the customer. Examples of dissatisfiers include bugs in the system, escalated problems, missing component, damaged product, late delivery, response time not met and so on.

Data from customers is gathered centrally and by utilizing SAS software an analysis of trends is done and reported and distributed world-wide. Action is then taken by all employees to reduce these dissatisfiers. A target is set to reduce these dissatisfiers and a number of initiatives are put in place to achieve this objective.

SunTeams (groups of employees) have been set up to generate projects to improve customer satisfaction. This way people can see the impact they make in improving customer satisfaction and their bonuses have been linked to achieving targeted reductions.

Customer Loyalty Index

In 1996 Sun introduced the Customer Loyalty Index which is designed as an external measurement of customer loyalty drivers. A total of eight surveys, conducted by an independent third party, will measure customer satisfaction, willingness to recommend Sun, willingness to repurchase from Sun and customer delight. This index is an enhancement of ongoing efforts to clearly understand Sun's customers. The Index is designed to tell Sun how customers feel about Sun.

Employee Quality Index

The Employee Quality Index is the sum of the number of times that 18 performance inhibitors (or roadblocks) occurred in a given week as perceived by Sun's employee population.

Managing Performance

The 18 roadblocks to employee performance are:

- Ineffective management skills
- Poorly planned or implemented organization
- Inadequate, missing or overly bureaucratic processes
- Product quality problems
- Work without customer value
- Poorly planned or executed project/programme
- Business strategy misunderstood
- Compensation issues
- Specific training unavailable.
- Not recognized for hard work and results
- Unavailable or difficult-to-use tools/applications
- No performance feedback
- Goals don't achieve right results
- Lack of co-operation/teamwork between groups
- Confusion/conflict between groups
- Career development unclear
- Responsibility without authority
- Key employee I depended on left Sun

The index is derived by collecting data from a weekly random sample survey of 750 Sun employees world-wide. This index does not measure an employee's satisfaction with or attitudes toward the company, the job, management, pay or co-workers.

Employee satisfaction rating

This trend line measures the rating employees give to the following five questions. It is designed to measure their satisfaction with Sun as an employer.

1. Overall, Sun is an enjoyable and satisfying place to work.
2. Working at Sun gives me a chance to work with exciting and challenging people.
3. I have a strong sense of pride and accomplishment in the work I do at Sun.
4. My supervisor manages me in a way that supports my success and increases my commitment to Sun.
5. There are enough opportunities for development/training, lateral transfer development projects, cross-training or promotion that I can foresee a continuing career with Sun.

The rating is done on a scale of 1 (definitely disagree) to 7 (definitely agree).

The Sun Quality Index is designed to reduce customer dissatisfiers (CQI) and employee performance inhibitors (EQI). By doing so Sun hopes to improve both customer and employee satisfaction. This will lead to the performance objectives Sun aspires to.

Customer satisfaction and employee satisfaction go hand in hand. According to Mike Roberts, "Quality starts with the employee, but is proven by the customer."

The attitude of employees matters very much in delivering service excellence. Customer satisfaction starts with employee satisfaction. Like nurses who feel very strongly they want to care for their patients, likewise employees should feel in their stomachs the desire to serve their customers well.

However, to have a feeling like that, employees themselves have to feel 'happy' in what they do and the way their organizations treat them. Organizations have to trust them and empower them to make appropriate decisions. Trust comes about when there is a series of positive encounters. Such positive encounters are characterized by allowing people to make mistakes (promoting a tolerant culture), empowering staff to make decisions, and fair treatment. It is said that to make a person trustworthy you have to trust him first.

A focus on the personal development of employees is going to be the key differentiating factor for successful and excellent organizations in the late 1990s and the twenty-first century. Winning performance is a matter of satisfying your customers' requirements and meeting their perceptions.

It is said that 'what the customer perceives, the customer must receive'. The five key elements of managing customer perception are:

■ Reliability
■ Assurance
■ Courtesy
■ Empathy
■ Trust

What do business executives think of service?

In 1992 Digital Equipment Co. in association with John Humble and Management Centre Europe undertook a survey of executive opinion in the United Kingdom on the theme of Service – The New Competitive Edge.

By 'service' they meant ". . . company's philosophy internally and externally and the policies, procedures and behaviours which provide products, sales and after sales support which meet customers' needs and expectations".

In response to the first two questions below, 5 = most important, 0 = least important.

How important is each factor in influencing your customers to buy your major product or service?

	Europe	USA	Japan	UK
Quality	4.4	4.3	4.5	4.3
Reliability	4.2	4.1	4.6	4.1
Problem solving	3.7	3.7	4.3	3.5
Price	3.4	2.6	4.1	3.5
Speed of delivery	3.4	3.7	3.7	3.4
Courtesy	3.1	3.8	4.3	3.4
After-sales service	3.4	3.3	3.9	3.3
Design	2.7	2.6	3.4	2.9
Guarantee	2.7	2.1	3.8	2.4
Packaging	2.2	2.3	2.9	2.1

Where is there most room for improvement in your organization?

	Europe	USA	Japan	UK
Quality	3.1	3.2	3.1	3.3
Speed of delivery	3.0	3.2	2.3	3.1
Courtesy	2.6	2.9	3.6	2.9
Problem solving	3.0	3.2	3.3	2.8
Reliability	2.6	2.8	3.2	2.8
After-sales service	2.7	3.1	3.1	2.7
Price	2.2	2.6	3.0	2.3
Design	2.1	2.6	2.8	2.2
Packaging	1.9	2.3	2.3	1.9
Guarantees	1.6	2.1	2.6	1.5

132

Performing for your customers

Do you think in the next 5 years that service to the customer will be more or less important?

	Europe %	USA %	Japan %	UK %
Much more important	69	69	88	73
More important	25	23	11	22
Same	4	7	1	5
Less important	1	1	0	0

(Source: Service – The New Competitive Edge. A Survey of UK Executive Opinion. Digital Equipment Company. 1992)

Corporate strategy and customer satisfaction

Examine the mission statement or strategic objective of your organization. Do you come across the word 'customer'? If  not, then your organization is not customer-focused and its chances of survival are not very high.

How would you write the mission statement of your organization?

_____

_____

_____

_____

_____

_____

Winning performance – Key success factors

- Your mission statement must incorporate meeting customer needs as a core objective.
- In formulating corporate objectives, do not miss out on explicitly mentioning managing customer perception and requirements as one of the key strategic objectives.
- At a departmental/divisional/team level highlight delivering service excellence as the objective of all operations.
- Install a mechanism to find out if customer needs are met or not (Figure 3.2).
- Incorporate employee performance monitoring within the customer needs control loop.
- Be a listening organization.
- Measure customer satisfaction, customer loyalty, customer defection.
- Reward staff for meeting and exceeding customer satisfaction.
- Analyse customer feedback properly and take appropriate action soon.
- Involve staff in coming up with suggestions to improve customer service.
- Train your staff in dealing with customers and in interpersonal communication.
- Benchmark against your competitors and other organizations to improve customer service.
- In recruiting staff consider delivering service excellence as one of the key criteria and competencies.
- Develop an empathetic relationship with your customers.
- Empower your staff to make decisions to address customers' problems on time.
- Deliver what you promise.
- Do not pay lip service to quality and customer service. It will backfire on your performance.
- Trust your staff to resolve problems.
- Provide strong leadership.
- Customer service is won in the trenches. Go and visit the trenches.
- Consider putting resources into customer service as an investment, not a cost.

Performing for your customers

- Customer expectation thresholds change, so monitor continuously.
- Set the customer, not the product, as the focal point of business activity.
- Treat customers as an appreciating asset.
- Strive for customer loyalty. Remember customer satisfaction is not loyalty. Loyalty is a combination of satisfaction, recommendation and repurchase.

If customers are satisfied they will continue giving you their business and you have their loyalty. There is bound to be a strong positive relationship between winning performance resulting in financial success and meeting customer satisfaction.

Selected reading

Cannie, J. and Caplin, D. (1991). *Keeping Customers For Life*. American Management Association.
Cook, S. (1992). *Customer Care*. Kogan Page.
Drucker, P. (1955). *The Practice of Management*. Butterworth-Heinemann.
Drucker, P. (1964). *Managing For Results*. Butterworth-Heinemann.
Drucker, P. (1987). *The Effective Executive*. Butterworth-Heinemann.
Moss Kanter, R. (1989). *When Giants Learn To Dance*. Simon & Schuster.
Peters, T. (1994). *In Pursuit of Wow*. Vintage Books.
Peters. T. and Waterman, R. Jr (1982). *In Search of Excellence*. Harper & Row.
Stewart, T. (1995). After all you've done for your customers, why are they still NOT HAPPY? *Fortune*, 11 December.
Vandermerwe, S. (1993). *From Tin Soldiers to Russian Dolls*. Butterworth-Heinemann.
Whiteley, R. (1995). *The Customer Driven Company*. Century.

6 Environmental performance

in brief

Shoot for the moon . . . even if you miss you'll be among the stars.
Unknown

Summary

■ Environmental considerations in business are commanding some attention. Organizations now want to go beyond legal requirements and adopt environmentally-friendly policies, products and processes.

■ Some organizations now (prompted by the Chartered Institute of Certified Accountants who initiated an award) produce annual environment reports.

■ The Eco-Audit Management System (EMAS) was introduced throughout the European Union in order to enable improvement of the environmental performance of organizations.

■ BS7750 is the UK standard for defining the scope and contents of an organization's environment management system.

■ The series of 1400 standards were introduced in 1996 to enhance environmental performance in business.

■ There is good evidence of companies reaping significant business benefits by adopting environmental focus policies. BT, British Airways, Norsk Hydro, Nissan, Vauxhall and other companies have achieved cost advantage by focusing on the environment.

■ In 1996 Business in the Environment published its first Index of Corporate Environment Engagement.

Environmental performance

■ Environmental concerns and requirements put pressure on companies to comply and come up with solutions. Such pressures have resulted in companies coming up with innovative solutions. Companies like ABB, Rhone Poulenc, Dow Chemical, Du Pont and ICI are investing in innovative technologies in order to achieve the best environmental performance.
■ Nissan pays attention to environmental performance.
■ How Electrolux avoided the 'green marketing' thrust.
■ The late 1990s and the early twenty-first century will witness the growth of benchmarking environmental management systems in order to adopt 'best practice'.

For a long time the environment remained at the periphery of organizational performance. Paying attention to environmental aspects of organizational performance meant incurring more cost without getting tangible returns which would have an impact on the bottom line.

According to the Council of Science and Technology Institute, in 1990 30 per cent of UK companies had formal environmental policies compared with 100 per cent of companies in Germany and 70 per cent in Ireland. Just under half of UK companies had a board member responsible for environmental management, compared with 75 per cent in Germany, 80 per cent in Denmark and 100 per cent in the Netherlands. In 1993 65 per cent of UK companies had designated managerial responsibility for environmental management issues. Gradually more and more companies are beginning to undertake environmental audits.

What is environmental auditing?

According to the definition of the International Chamber of Commerce (ICC), environmental auditing is

A management tool comprising a systematic documented periodic and objective evaluation of how well environmental organization, management and equipment are performing with the aim of helping to safeguard the environment by:

Managing Performance

(i) facilitating management control of environmental practices; and

(ii) assessing compliance with company policies which would include meeting regulatory requirements.

(ICC, 1988)

BS 7750 defines environmental management audit as:

A systematic evaluation to determine whether or not the environmental management system and the environmental performance it achieves conform to the planned arrangements, and whether or not the system is implemented effectively, and is suitable to fulfil the organization's environmental policy and objectives.

In the early 1990s there was an increased public awareness of green issues and many organizations began to respond to such awareness. Many organizations now consider environmental indicators as one of the key measures of their performance. At the second World Industry Conference on Environmental Management held in Rotterdam in April 1991, there were more than 7000 leading industrialists present to discuss key environmental issues affecting their businesses.

Green accounting

The early 1990s also saw the movement to promote corporate environmental disclosure. The Chartered Association of Certified Accountants established an annual environmental reporting awards scheme open to all UK companies. The scheme's judging panel consists of representatives from industry, the accounting profession, the trade unions, academia, the investment community and environmental groups.

The first recipients of the ACCA Environmental Reporting Award were British Airways and Norsk Hydro. British Airways' Environmental Review was related to the environmental effect of BA's operations and evaluating the company's environmental culture in terms of management attitudes, awareness and commitment to management issues.

The Norsk Hydro Environmental Report related to the manufacturing activities of the group in the United Kingdom. The report focused its attention on the group's manufacturing areas and their impact on environmental performance.

Environmental performance

The report identifies statutory regulations with which they have to comply and discloses performance against these regulations.

The rise of environmental management systems

The introduction of the Eco-Audit Management Scheme (EMAS) throughout the European Union has added an extra dimension for organizations seeking to use management systems in order to raise environmental awareness and improve business performance. EMAS is a voluntary scheme aimed at improving the environmental performance of organizations. To achieve recognition, companies must develop an environmental system and prepare a public environmental statement. Both must be validated by an independent accredited certification body.

BS 7750 is the UK standard for defining the scope and contents of an organization's Environmental Management System (EMS). The standard is voluntary and consists of the following elements:

■ Developing an environmental policy
■ Evaluating environmental effects
■ Setting overall goals and specific measurable targets
■ Reviewing the system regularly

In the autumn of 1996 a new standard derived from BS 7750 was introduced. This was ISO 14001. This is the first of a planned family of standards which will enable an organization to evaluate its environmental policies and practices with a view to enhancing its environmental performance.

The requirements of an ISO 14001 Environmental Management System are:

■ Top-level management commitment
■ Development of a policy and its communication to the public
■ Establishment of relevant legal and regulatory requirements

Managing Performance

- Development of environmental objectives and targets
- Establishment and maintenance of an environmental programme(s) in order to achieve its objectives and targets
- Implementation of a system including personnel training, documentation, operational control and emergency preparedness and response
- Monitoring and measurement of operational activities, including record keeping
- Development of procedures to prevent and correct any potential non-conformance within the system and in accordance with relevant legislation
- Audit procedures
- Management review to determine the system's availability, adequacy and effectiveness

Source: *European Quality*, **3**, No. 5, p. 15

Since February 1996 European organizations certified to BS 7750, whose business falls within the scope of the European Union's Eco-management and Audit scheme (EMAS) Regulation, have been able to use BS 7750 to meet most of the requirements for registration to EMAS.

Why should organizations be interested in adopting environmental management standards?

- Compliance with legislation
- To achieve cost savings
- To adhere to the supplier's requirements
- To enhance environmental performance
- Insurers take a favourable view in times of disaster
- In some cases mitigate liability
- Win stakeholders' confidence
- Marketing ploy
- Adopt best practice management

Examples of environmental performance

1. *The Financial Times* on 31 May 1995 reported Vauxhall, the UK arm of the US company General Motors, as the first recipient of an award for environmental management. The Vauxhall Ellesmere Port plant has become the first car factory to receive the BS 7750 award for environment management from the British Standards Institution. It acknowledges the management's environmental awareness. Shopfloor staff were trained and environmental responsibility was shifted to senior staff. Ten environmental auditors were appointed to monitor environmental progress. Most of the changes involved eliminating waste and reducing energy consumption.

2. The article 'Greening the bottom line', published in *Management Today* in July 1995, describes how Nissan, the Japanese car company, is attempting to become environmentally friendly: "The most vivid example of Nissan's policy in action is the way that money saved by recycling plastic off-cuts from the manufacture of Micra and Primera fuel tanks is paying for the switch to environmentally friendly (but more expensive) water-based paints on the Micra to reduce solvent emissions."

Environment is good for your business health: Nissan's story, by an insider

Nissan Motor Manufacturing (UK) Ltd, NMUK, was established in 1984 at Washington, in Sunderland in the North of England. It was the first Japanese car manufacturer to set up production in Europe. Two years later the plant produced its first vehicle, the Bluebird, a Japanese styled, designed and developed car, mainly from Japanese components.

In 1986 Nissan invested £50 million and today the investment stands at £1.25 billion. The 'New Primera', designed and developed in Europe, with more than 80 per cent of the vehicle of European content, has recently been launched.

Managing Performance

Nissan's focus on environmental performance is very well explained in the article 'No back-seat driving' which appeared in *Supply Management*, 5 September 1996. The article is by Robert Gray, Purchasing Manager with Nissan Motor Manufacturing UK.

Nissan Manufacturing UK's (NMUK) environmental journey began several years ago and, initially, was brought into focus by a need to comply with legislation. Achieving this soon brought all functions, including our suppliers, together on activities designed to meet requirements but at no on-cost. We achieved the legislative requirements on time and made cost savings that not only paid for the investment but allowed further investment towards other business needs.

An example of the activities initiated by Nissan is purchasing, packaging and components delivery. We were faced with many legislative demands, and the general business direction of improving the logistical chain, through rationalization, efficiency and improved quality.

We set out to look at it from the total business need. Foremost was the instruction to meet environmental legislation but at no cost. Achieving this requires savings to be made elsewhere to offset against legislative demands. First, we had to identify and understand all the drivers of the activity. A list was compiled including total detailed costs expended within each category. This involved collaboration with suppliers of components and packaging in order to detail and calculate all costs, including secondary costs.

For example, if we received components in cardboard box packaging from a supplier and our intention was to delete the cardboard and use a returnable stillage, we took not only the cost of the cardboard versus cost of new stillage but included such issues as time saved on decanting the cardboard box to present the components to the assembly line versus the ability to present the new stillage direct to lineside. Also, by working with the supplier of the component, we calculated any benefits in their manufacturing and used those to reduce the piece cost.

Also, eliminating decanting operations improved the welfare of employees by reducing heavy lifting operations. This reduces potential for industrial sickness which is a cost to the company.

In Nissan's first stages of its improved packaging measures, we realized advantages such as reduced piece price and handling and improved presentation, as well as meeting environmental needs. Money was saved as well. In 1994, a single activity of this nature created an annual savings of £95,500 for an investment of £127,800. Savings to date are now several millions.

A further example is dealing with safe transportation of airbags. An airbag contains explosives which are subject to handling and transportation legislation. There are also environmental issues should there be an incident in transit. Our initial packaging was aimed at meeting those issues. However, it was expensive and created waste from the protection involved. The new method for delivery was developed jointly with the supplier. The benefits it will bring are:

- elimination of supplier packaging (environmental waste);
- reduction of disposable packaging (waste);
- improved compliance with legislation on transportation of hazardous goods (environmental issues);
- elimination of decanting operations (safety and cost);
- prevention of dust ingress (quality improvement);
- reduced handling requirements (safety, employee welfare).

We have also worked on other issues with suppliers, such as recycling (for example, of plastic fuel tanks), reduction of process waste, paint technology and elimination of environmentally unsound materials. All achieved reduced costs.

The environment is best dealt with not as a specialized activity, but as a natural part of business. It is not an obstacle to performance but an important driver in obtaining business advantages. The public do not buy items solely because they are green; they buy them because they are better quality and lower cost as well as green.

According to Robert Gray, Manager – Purchasing, at Nissan, "At NMUK we have viewed environment issues not as a standalone set of rules or requirements that must be complied with but as a business opportunity, as a driver in obtaining business benefit and advantage and to that end we believe we have been successful. However, we have also looked at our community responsibilities to the environment also.

"It was Nissan's intention from the outset that plant would not affect the surrounding areas and we have taken steps jointly with Sunderland Borough Council to ensure this.

Managing Performance

During our site building we constructed a catchment reservoir, adjacent to Barmston Pond which is owned by the local authority, to enable the water levels to be kept at the correct level to encourage wild fowl to visit. Which is why today skylarks fly over the factory and wild geese wade in a wild fowl habitat beside the factory. A far cry from the industrial picture of smoke-belching chimneys and slag heaps of years ago."

TIME OUT

Does your organization focus on environmental performance?

If yes, outline three examples of environmental performance.

_____

_____

_____

If not, consider three areas which could be considered by your organization in improving environmental performance.

_____

_____

_____

Electrolux and the environment

Following is an excerpt from an article in *PRISM*, published by Arthur D. Little, Inc.

Electrolux avoided the 'green marketing' thrust of the 1980s, choosing instead to take a deeper and longer-term approach to integrating environmental issues into business processes. This route holds much greater promise of sustained advantage from lower costs and increased revenues. For example, the company is piloting several studies in which it is selling functionality rather than physical products. The Euroclean division, which has traditionally developed, manufactured, and sold commercial floor cleaning products, is developing a business strategy of offering the customer the cleaning capacity. This capacity, guaranteed in terms of function and quality, is paid for on a monthly basis. Electrolux Euroclean remains the owner of the equipment, and the company's role switches from manufacturing to the service sector.

Why move in this direction? For two main reasons. First it enables Electrolux to retain tighter control of its proprietary technology, thereby giving the company a competitive edge at a time when innovative modular products using less material and parts will create market advantage. Second, Electrolux can stay at the forefront in meeting product take-back and recycling demands, soon to be legislated in many European (and other) countries. While this change may be essential for the future health of the company, it shows how concern for the environment can be a motor of change in an organization. To achieve a successful business based on function, Electrolux, which is traditionally strong in manufacturing, will need to acquire new skills in marketing and selling services.

Measurement of performance

Enlightened companies are linking environmental performance to strategic and other performance indicators for the business as a whole and for individual product lines or subsidiaries. But companies seeking to truly measure the impact of their operations and products on the environment face stiff challenges. For example, most of the present-day environmental measures do not measure product performance over a lifetime of 10 to 20 years. Moreover, environmental issues can be extremely complex and difficult to separate from product performance. A good example is a dishwasher that cleans dishes better and uses only 15 litres of water instead of 45 litres. One effective way to overcome these measurement issues is to focus on true business measures, with environmental measurement designed in as part of these. The environmental 'measures' can range from a factory's energy costs to the goodwill generated from development of an effective lawnmower that is solar powered.

The measures that Electrolux uses to monitor success in meeting targets are the logical result of the company's holistic approach to environmental management as part of the business process. In short, the company has developed three product-related measuring tools that are linked to its economic progress:

- The share of leading environmentally sound products
- Product improvements from year to year
- Practical recycling possibilities

Recognizing the direct link between the company's environmental strategy and financial results, Electrolux management defines two ways to create value. The first is gross profit and net sales, which hinges on the value of products to customers as well as on reduced costs because of improved process efficiency. The other is corporate goodwill and brand value, assets that show up on the balance sheet.

(This discussion of Electrolux, and of the measurement of environmental performance in general, is printed by permission from 'Environmental Performance and Business Success – The Electrolux Experience' by Jonathan B. Shopley and Howard B. Ross, *Prism*, Fourth Quarter 1996, published by Arthur D. Little, Inc. pp. 67–9.)

Business in the Environment

Business in the Environment (BiE) was set up in 1989 to promote environmental challenges facing all businesses today. It helps all types of businesses in practical terms to adopt methodologies to improve and enhance environmental performance. The board of BiE consists of twelve of the largest UK companies.

It perceives environmental consideration to be not an appendix to business strategy and planning, but one of the core components.

It published its first Index of Corporate Environmental Engagement on 18 November 1996 in the hope that it will become an annual feature. The companies from the FTSE-100 were asked questions on environmental policy, systems and practice.

They produced the following league table:

How green is my company?

1st quintile	2nd quintile	3rd quintile	4th quintile	5th quintile
British Airways	Allied Domecq	Argos	Abbey National	Bass
BT	Asda Group	Bank of Scotland	Barclays	Burmah Castrol
Enterprise Oil	BAA	Blue Circle Indus.	Br. Aerospace	Burton
ICI	BAT Industries	Boots	Cable & Wireless	Commercial Union
Marks & Spencer	BP	British Gas	Cadbury-Schweppes	General Accident
National Power	British Steel	Courtaulds	Carlton Comms	Granada
Nat West Bank	GEC	Glaxo Wellcome	Dixons	Gt. Universal Stores
RTZ Corporation	Grand Metropolitan	Guinness	Kingfisher	Land Securities
Safeway Stores	Hanson	National Grid	Ladbroke	Rank Organization
Scottish Power	J. Sainsbury	P&O Steam Nav.	Legal & General	Reuters Holdings
Shell Transport & Trad.	Lasmo	Pilkington	Reckitt & Coleman	Royal Bank of Scot.
Smithkline Beecham	PowerGen	Redland	RMC	Royal & Sun Alliance
Thames Water	Severn Trent	Southern Electric	Rolls-Royce	Scottish & Newcastle
Unilever	Smith & Nephew	Tate & Lyle	United Utilities	Tesco
	Thorn-EMI		3i Group	TI Group

Absolute score;
% of total points

| 83–94 | 69–82 | 57–68 | 47–56 | 3–42 |

Source: Business in the Environment 1996.

Managing Performance

In 1995 Management Centre Europe, the European HQ of the American Management Association, undertook a survey on 'Business and the Environment'. A total of 723 responses were returned. Eleven per cent were chief executives, 43 per cent top managers, 32 per cent middle managers and the rest specialist functions. Twenty-eight per cent worked in general management, 27 per cent in marketing, 12 per cent in human resources and the rest in a cross-section of disciplines.

Following are snapshots of their findings:

- Sixty per cent of respondents felt their organizations were concerned and active in relation to the environment.
- Fifty-two per cent said that their company had "an environmental charter or rule book that was given to employees" (with the British and Irish reporting the highest incidence – 59 per cent, and southern Europe the lowest – 38 per cent.
- Fifty-four per cent said that their organization had "published a report (or included a section in their annual report) that highlights their concerns for environmental issues."
- Over 66 per cent said that their company had "carried out an environmental audit", again with a high score from Britain and Ireland – 71 per cent.
- Thirty-nine per cent said that environmental initiatives were driven by the CEOs but few CEOs took charge of environmental committees.
- About 33 per cent said that their organizations actually had given real, on-the-ground practical training and development.
- Nearly 90 per cent felt it was important for business professionals to have training on environmental issues.

The survey report concludes: "While there are distinct signs that business is aware of the environmental issues, is even cynical about the way it has been abused by some as a marketing tool, there is still much to be done, particularly in the adoption and creation of awareness programmes that give employees better understanding of the relationship between the environment and the products or services their organization offers."

(Source: Business and Environment Survey 1995, Management Centre Europe)

Environmental performance

How green is your organization? Identify three areas of your organization where you can give examples of environmental focus.

1 . . . .

2 . . . .

3 . . . .

Environmental messages from management thinkers

For a long time businesses did not pay much attention to environmental factors and performance. The environment was considered to be the preoccupation of 'lefties' and 'softies'. There was also a very strong view held by business managers that improving environmental factors within the business context would increase private costs and make business less competitive. The arguments presented are similar to the arguments presented by those who oppose the adoption of the Social Chapter.

Figure 6.1 shows that in order to improve environmental performance the private costs will increase which will make it very difficult for businesses to gain competitive advantage. In the article by Michael E. Porter (the strategy 'guru') and

Figure 6.1 Private costs vs. environmental benefits

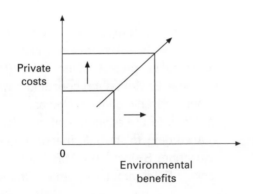

Managing Performance

Claas van der Linde entitled 'Green and Competitive – ending the Stalemate', published in the September–October 1995 issue of the *Harvard Business Review*, the authors state:

- In the present changing competitive environment it is important for organizations to be on their toes and find innovative solutions.
- Legislative requirements in relation to environment have been blessings in disguise in 'forcing' companies to come up with innovative solutions.
- Innovation enhances competitiveness.
- Customers bear the costs when they use products that pollute or waste energy. Designing pollution-preventing schemes and policies will have a favourable impact on costs.
- They give examples of companies like Dow Chemical, Rhone Poulenc, Du Pont and others which have made significant efforts in reducing waste, using by-products which were originally incinerated, and investing in pollution-preventing technologies and thus gained significant cost advantage.
- These companies responded positively to the pressures of environmental regulation. The dynamic thinking and mindset of these companies prompted innovative solutions and enhanced their competitiveness in the marketplace.
- The authors write that "managers must start to recognize environmental improvement as an economic and competitive opportunity, not as an annoying cost or an inevitable threat.
- "Today globlization is making the notion of comparative advantage obsolete. Companies can source low-cost inputs anywhere and new, rapidly emerging technologies can offset disadvantages in the cost of inputs."

Today many companies are working together to encourage environmentally based innovations. A good example of a collaborative project is the MIBE (Managing the Industrial Business Environment) consortium which is IMD's company-sponsored environmental research consortium. MIBE helps to integrate the environment into daily decision making.

According to the information provided by IMD, based in Lausanne, Switzerland, MIBE came up with two integrating tools: Environmetrics and Green Standard Bearers.

Environmental performance

"Environmetrics puts metrics on environmental considerations translating them into the language of business and Green Standard Bearers are individuals within companies who encourage other employees to care about the environment, influence others to change to more environmentally sensitive practices, and develop sustainable products and ideas for eliminating the use of hazardous materials."

Environmental performance and the ISO 14000 series

In 1991 the International Organization for Standardization (ISO) established a Strategic Advisory Group on Environment (SAGE) to investigate all the areas of environmental management and performance where the development of international standards might be beneficial to the business community.

In 1993 ISO set up a technical committee to develop the standards proposed by SAGE. The core and the supporting standards covering different areas and aspects of environmental management were allocated numbers in the range of 14000 to 14099 and are now popularly referred to as 'the 14000 Series'.

Of central importance in the ISO 14000 series are the environmental management system (EMS) standards ISO 14001 and ISO 14004. These standards allow an organization to proactively and systematically evaluate how its activities, products and services interact with the environment and how improvements in overall environmental performance can be achieved.

Organizations implementing an ISO 14001 EMS can secure a range of potential trade-related and financial benefits and may improve their competitive edge in a number of ways. For example, by:

■ Achieving improvements in overall environmental performance
■ Reducing raw material and energy usage
■ Identifying alternative, 'cleaner' manufacturing processes and materials
■ Identifying waste minimization opportunities
■ Meeting certification criteria imposed by vendor organizations in contractual specifications
■ Acting in a proactive manner to minimize exposure to environmental liabilities, thereby reducing insurance premiums and incidences of non-compliance with legislation

Managing Performance

■ Enhancing their corporate environmental image, meeting consumer expectations and thus improving market share
■ Improving internal communication with staff members and contractors and external relations with the local community, the general public and government at every level
■ Improved access to external ethical/environmental investment funding and internal corporate funding
■ Increasing the likelihood of successful planning applications and pollution control consents/permits

ISO 14001, like BS7750, uses the Deming Plan 'Do, Check, Act' cycle to develop and improve environmental performance.

Source: Edited version of Environmental Council Article, 'The ISO 14000 Series – Overview and Current Status'. Written by Mark Barthel, Product Manager, Environmental Management Systems, BSI Training Services.

Industry's response to ISO 14001

According to information provided by Mark Barthel, Product Manager, Environmental Management Systems, BSI Training Services, the Institut Supérieur de Commerce International à Dunkerque surveyed organizations to evaluate their experience of the ISO 14001 standard.

The Institute's study involved more than five hundred companies in France, the Netherlands and the UK (56 per cent of the companies involved in this study were from the manufacturing sector and 44 per cent were from the service sector). The study revealed that 80 per cent of the respondents found that being certified to an EMS standard was cost-effective, with 75 per cent prepared to recommend the process to others.

When asked what factors influenced them to seek certification to ISO 14001 the respondents highlighted the following:

■ Compliance with legislative requirement (81%)
■ Improved market share (80%)
■ Customer pressure (78%)
■ Public recognition (64%)

Benchmarking and environmental performance

In the 1980s and 1990s benchmarking became very popular among many organizations. Benchmarking is a change programme which enables the achievement of the 'best practice'. Rank Xerox defines benchmarking as "a continuous systematic process of evaluating companies recognized as industry leaders, to determine business and work processes that represent 'best practice' and establish performance goals".

Some companies got together to form benchmarking clubs in order to facilitate comparisons of best-practice processes in the areas of customer service, finance, total quality, leadership and the strategy formulation process.

Environmental performance will achieve significant importance in the late 1990s and in the new millennium. It will become one of the key aspects of managerial responsibilities. Since we now have the first ever Index of Corporate Environmental Engagement published by Business in the Environment, it will be easier to look at the league table and conduct benchmarking exercises in relation to the 'best practice' environmental management system.

For example, Kingfisher, in the fourth quintile, can benchmark against Marks & Spencer, in the first quintile, or Cable & Wireless (fourth quintile) can benchmark against BT (first quintile).

Benchmarking involves the following steps:

1. Seek top management support and involvement.
2. First determine what aspect of environmental management system you want to benchmark against. Do you want to consider the complete system or only one aspect of the system?
3. Identify which company either in your own sector (e.g. oil producing or energy or retail etc.) or another sector has the reputation of adopting 'best practice'.
4. Gather information on that company. Information can be obtained from different sources, e.g. from the company itself, from Business in the Environment, British Standards Institute, specialist consultants, libraries etc.

Managing Performance

5. Analyse the data you have gathered and relate it to your own practice. Determine performance gaps.
6. Formulate an environmental policy with a view to adopting 'best practice'.
7. Conduct a resources budget and analysis to implement a 'best practice' policy.
8. Communicate the project to all staff. Ask for suggestions and involvement.
9. Work out the Deming cycle approach of 'Plan-Do-Act'.
10. Monitor the whole process continuously.

The sooner companies start benchmarking and adopting 'best practice' in environmental management and performance the sooner they will sustain their competitive advantage and will be performing like organizations of the twenty-first century.

In his speech at the 8th Round table with the Government of Italy, organized by the Economist Conferences and Business International, Italy, in November 1996, the European commissioner said:

> Benchmarking at enterprise level can offer a key instrument for improving competitiveness. It remains the primary responsibility of industry to implement such benchmarking and it is not the intention of the European Commission to become involved in the benchmarking of individual enterprises. However, a number of schemes, both public and private seek to promote benchmarking of enterprises to a wider audience, particularly to small and medium sized enterprises that do not have the resources or the experience to undertake benchmarking on their own.

Environmental efficiency was highlighted as one of the key priority areas for performance in *Commission Communication*. It says:

> Benchmarking of environmental efficiency will be required to ensure that efforts to improve competitiveness are not made at the expense of sustainability. Key criteria relate to the capacity of the economy to efficiently transform flows of materials into goods and services. Suitable indicators in the field of energy efficiency already exist. However, benchmarks for other material flows, such as the use of water, which is becoming an increasingly rare

resource, will need to be developed. Criteria such as recycling rates of water can help to measure the efficiency with which the European economy in general and European industry in particular is using resources.

Caution: Benchmarking is not about copying the practice or the system. It is about adopting and adapting in order to achieve 'best practice'. It is about understanding how 'best practice' comes about.

Selected reading

CSTI Environmental Information Paper 2 (1994). Environmental Auditing. Prepared by the CSTI Advisory Committee on the Environment.
Financial Times Survey (1996). Environment: Management and Technology. 21 June.
Financial Times (1996). Polluting industries marked by index. 18 November.
International Institute for Management Development (1996). Perspectives for Manager, **2**, No. 8, September.
Kermally, S. (1996). *Total Management Thinking*. Butterworth-Heinemann.
Management Centre Europe Survey (1995). Business and the Environment.
Porter, M. and van der Linde, C. (1995). Green and Competitive – Ending the Stalemate. *Harvard Business Review*, September–October.
(Information on the 14001 series can be obtained from British Standards Institute, 389 Chiswick High Street, London, W4 4AL)

7

Corporate culture – performance context

in brief

Of all the things you wear, your expression is the most important.
Unknown

Summary

■ Corporate culture provides the context within which business decisions are made and implemented.

■ Corporate culture simply is 'the way we do business over here'. It encompasses the beliefs, values, norms and behaviours of the organization.

■ 'The way we do things over here' impacts upon the behaviour and performance of all employees and subsequently the performance of the total organization.

■ Corporate culture can be categorized into collaborative or co-operative or co-existence cultures. There are no good or bad cultures – there are only different cultures.

■ Many organizations like Levi Strauss, Johnson & Johnson, Federal Express and so on articulate their cultures via their aspiration or mission statements.

■ Cultural change is leveraged by TQM, Benchmarking, Business Process Re-engineering, Empowerment, Customer-focus and other change initiatives.

■ Initiatives taken by Rank Xerox, ICL, Miliken, DHL and IBM reflect the role of each management thinking in bringing about cultural change.

■ Corporate values are key to management change.

■ The findings of the survey on corporate values by Digital Equipment Company.

■ What is the meaning and the significance of value?

■ Values in relation to employment rights, management by intimidation, corporate bullying, stress at work and discrimination.

■ Changing the corporate culture – slow approach or shock therapy.

An organization operates within the context of its culture and values which, in turn, affects its performance. There are no good or bad cultures as such. Different organizations have different cultures.

The management world is awash with talk of corporate culture. It is important at the outset to define and explain the concept of 'culture'.

What is culture?

Sociologists relate culture to the totality of what is learned by individuals and members of society. According to Edward Taylor, an anthropologist, "culture is that complex whole which includes knowledge, belief, art, morals, law, custom, and any other capabilities acquired by man as a member of society". It refers to the standards, beliefs and attitudes in terms of which people act.

When you are on holiday and if you ask the natives of the countries in question why they observe certain rituals or why they dress in a certain manner or why they behave in a specific fashion towards certain groups of people, for example the elderly, they would say: "This is the way we do things here." Culture, therefore, constitutes a major driver towards individual and social behaviour.

A cultural value is a widely held belief about what is important to the community's identity or well-being. Communities and societies are made up of relations between people and groups and those relations are guided by cultural values.

Most of culture is pervasive; it is taken for granted. Cultural assumptions underline thought and action and culture touches every aspect of life.

What is corporate culture?

The concept of culture has been applied to organizations. Some management thinkers and writers have compared organizations to societies and they have attempted to explain the behaviour, action and performance of people working within organizations as a culture prevailing within an organization – corporate culture.

Corporate culture is defined as shared assumptions, beliefs, values and norms of the organization in so far as these drive shared patterns of behaviour. Corporate culture is 'the way we do things in our organization'. The way we do things impacts the performance of every individual and subsequently the performance of the organization as a whole.

Corporate culture affects:
- the way corporate strategies are formulated;
- the way membership of a board is constituted;
- the way business heads are promoted;
- the way business units are run;
- the way employees are selected;
- the way employees are inducted;
- the way performance is measured;
- the way customers are treated;
- the way trust is promoted within an organization;
- the way employees treat one another;
- the way employees are treated by top and senior management;
- the way employees are rewarded;
- the way decisions are made within organizations;
- the way employees are empowered;
- the way decisions, policies, values and strategies are communicated throughout the organization;
- the way leadership is exercised from the top.

In other words, everything that an organization does is the reflection of its culture, 'the way we do things here'.

Do you know the culture of your organization?

In most organizations there are layers of cultures. There is an outside ring as perceived by 'outsiders'. There is another ring as perceived by top management – "We have a culture of high performance, honesty and tolerance" or "We put our people first." There is another ring as perceived by senior management and yet another ring as perceived by employees – "This company does not care enough about us". Or "In some departments and some areas you can get away with murder."

As you peel or penetrate these various layers you begin to understand the different perceptions of various groups of employees and their resultant motivation and behaviour.

As one employee of a publishing company put it to me: "My company has two cultures – projected culture and real culture." Projected culture is designed to impress stakeholders who are outside the company. Then there is a real culture within what he called a Masonic ring. Various behaviours are tolerated and employees within this inner ring support each other. Promotions take place within this ring. There are other employees who belong to the projected culture segment (see Figure 7.1) whose behaviours are tolerated but they do not get anywhere professionally because their faces do not fit. The segment representing the projected culture becomes the house of **Silent Sabotage**. Their actions have an unfavourable impact on organizational performance. Every opportunity they get, they try to foul-mouth their organizations.

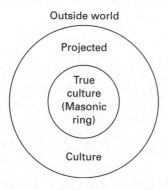

Figure 7.1 Dimensions of corporate culture

Managing Performance

Corporate culture can be categorized into:

■ **Collaborative culture**. In such a culture the degree of sociability and solidarity of employees is very high and as a consequence the performance of an organization as a whole is effective.
■ **Co-operative culture**. In such a culture the employees do co-operate but the degree of interpersonal effectiveness is low or not very high. The lack of sociability reduces the effectiveness of organizational performance.
■ **Co-existence culture**. In such a culture different groups (finance, marketing and sales, production etc.) tolerate each other's existence but the degree of sociability and solidarity is low. Groups try to work independently of one another. In such a culture organizational performance is adversely affected.
■ **Conflict culture**. In such a culture different groups are in conflict with each other and the organization as a whole lacks values and direction. Organizational performance is low and if no action is taken soon market forces will eliminate such an organization.

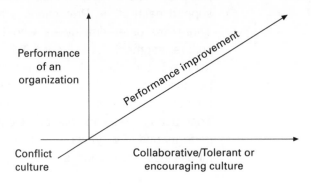

Figure 7.2 Organizational culture and performance effectiveness

Corporate culture – performance context

"The way we do things in my organization."
Highlight five aspects of your business that reflect the culture of your organization.

1. _____
   _____
   _____

2. _____
   _____
   _____

3. _____
   _____
   _____

4. _____
   _____
   _____

5. _____
   _____
   _____

How one company has translated its culture to bring about preferred behaviour

Levi Strauss has recently received very favourable publicity in terms of the way it treats its customers and employees. Here is an abstract of what they aspire to.

New behaviours

Management must exemplify "directness, openness to influence, commitment to the success of others, and willingness to acknowledge our own contributions to problems."

Managing Performance

Diversity

Levi's "values a diverse workforce (age, sex, ethnic group, etc.) of all levels of the organization . . . Differing points of view will be sought; diversity will be valued and honesty rewarded, not suppressed."

Recognition

Levi's will "provide greater recognition – both financial and psychic – for individuals and teams that contribute to our success . . . those who create and innovate and those who continually support day-to-day business requirements."

Ethical management practices

Management should epitomize "the stated standards of ethical behaviour. We must provide clarity about our expectations and must enforce these standards throughout the corporation."

Communications

Management must be "clear about company, unit, and individual goals and performance. People must know what is expected of them and receive timely, honest feedback . . ."

Empowerment

Management must "increase the authority and responsibility of those closest to our products and customers. By actively pushing the responsibility, trust and recognition into the organization, we can harness and release the capabilities of all our people."

Data: Levi Strauss & Co.
(Source: *Business Week*, 12 September 1994)

Levi believes their aspiration statement reflects their preferred culture. They hope their aspiration will guide the behaviour of their employees at every level and thus make Levi a successful company.

Levi has always valued its employees as long as they align their own aspirations with that of the company. They have always adopted a paternalistic attitude towards their employees. In 1906 they retained their employees on the payroll after an earthquake devastated the sewing factory and headquarters in San Francisco. In 1930 during the Great Depression, the company retained employees in spite of falling demand. Levi believes "the quality of our employees' lives is just as important as the quality of our products".

How do companies in practice leverage cultural change?

Many organizations leverage their corporate culture or change their corporate culture by introducing various change initiatives either from desperation or from reaction to competitive pressures. In other words, out of necessity. The key avenues used by many organizations to bring about cultural change have been the following:

- Introducing a total quality management initiative
- Becoming customer-focused
- Re-engineering their businesses
- Empowering their employees
- Forming cross-functional teams

Total quality management

In the 1980s many organizations introduced a total quality management (TQM) initiative in order to remain a player in a competitive market. TQM was one of the most pervasive aspects of management thinking.

Juran and Deming, the two most influential quality gurus, emphasized the need and the importance of commitment, communication, training and trust in people in achieving qualitative improvements throughout organizations.

In America the Malcolm Baldrige National Quality Award was instituted in 1987 to encourage organizations to adopt total quality management principles. The focus of the award is on organizations achieving specific qualitative standards in leadership, information and analysis, strategic planning, human resource development and management, process management and customer focus.

In Europe, the European Foundation for Quality Management which was founded in 1988 launched the annual European Quality Award in 1992. The award put specific emphasis on leadership, people management, policy and strategy, resources and processes. These are the 'enablers' within organizations that drive desired business results.

TQM and change in corporate culture – some examples

Rank Xerox UK

Rank Xerox launched a world-wide programme in 1989 called 'Leadership Through Quality'. The company achieved corporate transformation by focusing on recruitment and selection, reward, training, communication, senior management behaviour and standards and measurement. The director of quality and communication categorized enablers of transformation and quality achievement as 'open honest communication, organizational reflection and learning, and process improvement'.

TQM policy means managers are expected to hire and promote exponents of 'leadership through quality', seek and act on feedback and recognize and reward effective application of 'quality through leadership'. The emphasis throughout is on behaviour and performance.

ICL

At ICL a quality initiative began in 1986 and over the years it has gone through three stages, each with a focus of its own.

Stage one began in 1986 with a focus on quality conformance – Do It Right First Time. There was very little ownership of the initiative at line managers' level.

At stage two the focus changed to customer care. Measures and processes were restructured to change the corporate culture to focus on customers. Line managers experienced some ownership of the programme.

At stage three the focus changed to self-assessment using the model of the European Quality Foundation. Progress has been fast and there is total ownership of the quality programme at all levels.

Corporate culture – performance context

Miliken Industrials

Miliken has been working on total quality management for 15 years. The initiative began in 1981 with a narrow focus on improving the quality of the products. Subsequently, due to the influence of Tom Peters, the definition of quality was broadened to incorporate customer focus. This shifted the focus from the internal to the external perspective.

Gradually over time the ideas of other quality gurus were taken on board. Now quality means 'the use of all aspects of total quality to delight customers and thus ensure survival and long-term profitable growth'.

Along with quality initiatives many organizations like Motorola, ABB, Canon Europe, Avis, DHL and so on began to turn their attention to delivering service excellence and becoming customer-driven companies. The slogan of the early 1990s was not just to satisfy customers but to delight them. Various books, surveys and research began to focus attention on customers.

Companies took heed of the importance of customers and they introduced the following measures to listen to customers and to bring the voice of customers into their organizations:

- **Customer focus group**: A panel of customers is formed to give their opinion on the company and their competitors' products. Customers are invited to discuss a particular topic, for example, delivery of service.
- **Visits to customers**: Managers and cross-functional groups of employees were encouraged to visit customers to ascertain customers' needs and expectations.
- **Customer councils**: Organizations formed councils consisting of customers who would advise on products and their attributes.
- **Questionnaires/postal surveys**
- **Customer research** to ascertain key accounts, growth prospects and degree of relationship they have with the company.
- **Customer care training**.

Customer focus and impact on corporate culture: Some examples

DHL International (UK)

DHL is the world's largest carrier employing some 34 000 people in 222 countries around the world. Its customer base is as diverse as commerce itself. When things were not going well DHL decided to do away with functional allocation of responsibilities and created mini-businesses at the lowest possible level in order to take decision making closer to customers. In the process the company eliminated several layers of management, moving from a structure where the managing director was seven levels away from the courier to one today where he is four levels away.

Understanding customers, listen and learn are the watchwords at DHL. The company invests heavily in research to gain in-depth understanding of their customers' needs.

Another aspect of becoming customer-focused is managing the customers you have. At DHL the company has instituted a 'cradle to grave' policy. This is an approach to communication planning which is responsive to the current requirements and potential of a customer as their relationship with a supplier grows. The policy is designed to establish where in the customer life cycle DHL is currently sitting and to tailor communications precisely to address that position.

ICL

ICL's quality and customer-focus drive started from a crisis precipitated by IBM. It was very much a product-driven company. In 1981 ICL's losses reached £130 million. It was forced to go to the UK Government for loan guarantees to stay in business. Robert Wilmott took over as managing director and he began to transform the company. He changed the corporate culture from being product-driven to market and customer-driven. This meant change of management, change of product range, change of attitude and change of behaviour. Layers of bureaucracy vanished along with layers of middle management.

Wilmot's successor, Peter Bonfield, transformed ICL into a quality culture organization. He was confronted with massive resistance. He deployed organization-wide initiatives to wake up every employee to the need for proactive thinking.

The fundamental change was that of attitude. The company changed its focus from products to customers as its business emphasis shifted from manufacturing and supplying mainframes, minis, personal computers and software to system integration. Bonfield put the whole company into the mode of 'change culture'.

IBM and customer focus

In the cover story of *Business Week* of 9 December 1996, 'How IBM Became a Growth Company Again', it was stated that IBM was healthier than it had been in years. Customers were expected to spend £58.3 billion with IBM in 1996, a jump of 8 per cent from $54 billion in 1995.

According to *Business Week*, "IBM has arrived at this happy juncture by doing lots of things right since chairman and chief executive Louis V. Gerstner Jr. took over three and a half years ago. But the secret to IBM's success isn't great technology, cut-throat pricing or flashy marketing moves. It's approaching double-digit growth for the first time in almost seven years for one main reason. Under Gerstner, IBM has gone back to the most basic notion of how to succeed in business, talking to customers, learning their needs, and figuring out how to satisfy them ... Gerstner told *Business Week*: "I came here with a view that you start the day with customers, that you start thinking about the company around its customers, and you organize around customers". ... By his reckoning, Gerstner still spends 40% of his time with customers ..."

Changing the focus of business strategy to meet competitive needs impacts corporate structure

In the late 1990s the emphasis has shifted from winning and satisfying customers to retaining customers and winning their loyalty. According to Bain & Co, a management consulting company, a five per cent increase in customer retention can significantly increase profitability. A study conducted by Price Waterhouse showed that a two per cent increase in customer retention has the same profit impact as a ten per cent reduction in overheads.

Customer loyalty means sustaining the changes initiated in relation to values, beliefs, attitude, in other words sustaining changes in corporate culture. Customer loyalty means your existing customers are happy with the service you provide to the extent that they recommend your company to others and they continue purchasing from your company. Building a long-term relationship with customers means sustaining the focus adopted as far as corporate strategy is concerned.

Re-engineering

Business Process Re-engineering (BPR) wreaked havoc on the corporate culture of some organizations. In some cases it eliminated overnight the trust, beliefs and self-confidence of the employees in organizations. It created confusion about the notion 'This is the way we do things here.' People began to feel "We do not know what is happening here" or "We do not know any more how we do things over here."

Business Process Re-engineering as a management concept and thinking was introduced by Michael Hammer and Jim Champy in their book *Re-engineering the Corporation* published in 1993. BPR is a fundamental rethinking and radical redesign of business processes to achieve 'quantum leap' improvements in business results.

To Hammer and Champy, BPR means throwing away all the historical hang-ups, policy manuals and existing assumptions and starting from scratch. Many companies jumped on the bandwagon of BPR in order to achieve desired improvements in their business results.

Dramatic improvements were gained by companies like Reuters, IBM, Continental Canada Insurance, Ford Motor, AT&T Global Business, Hall Mark, American Express, Procter & Gamble and the like. Re-engineering initiatives meant re-orientation of corporate culture.

Hall Mark, for example, made people believe that change is a never-ending process and employees were made to believe that they make a difference and that employees don't do something because they simply said they would – they do it only if it still makes sense.

Taco Bell created customer focus and viewed re-engineering as a continuous process, and created a mentality of 'change begets change'.

The focus of BPR is on process. Processes in business are categorized into 'core' processes and 'support' processes. A core process creates value by the capabilities it gives the company from competitiveness. In practice it is alleged that many companies have a mismatch between business processes and the voice of the customer. There are many activities incorporated into the processes that have entered the business over time and that do not add value for the customers. Re-engineering eliminates non-value-adding processes and as a consequence an organization is streamlined and gets closer to its customers.

Some organizations adopted the banner of re-engineering to downsize their operations. Others did not invest enough thinking, time and resources to effect re-engineering properly. In some cases there was a lack of understanding of the implications of re-engineering and effective leadership. As a consequence, re-enginering created havoc as far as corporate culture was concerned.

Empowerment

Total quality management initiatives, making organizations customer-driven, re-engineering – all these new management concepts necessitated taking business decision making closer to customers, in other words changing the **corporate mindset**. Empowerment became one of the key management buzzwords in the early 1990s.

Empowerment meant pushing decision making down to the coal face and enabling employees to work as corporate entrepreneurs. Empowerment is defined as an act of releasing human energy. It is about creating situations where workers share power and assume the responsibility of making decisions for the benefit of the organizations they represent.

Empowerment can be looked at from a corporate perspective and an individual perspective. From a corporate perspective, effective empowerment can only take place if the focus is put on culture change. **The key element of empowerment is trust**. Organizations have to trust their employees to take responsibility for making decisions. Management guru Richard Pascale believes that values and trust (key components of corporate culture) are pre-conditions of empowerment. Theses two factors encourage individuals to think, experiment and improve. Empowerment transforms commitment into contribution.

Managing Performance

At an individual level, empowerment becomes effective if an individual wants responsibility, wants to own a problem, has the competence to resolve problems and feels trusted.

Empowerment requires a culture of service, commitment, respect, open communication, trust and tolerance. Organizations which have successfully empowered their employees have created an organizational climate (appropriate corporate culture) conducive to success.

Teaming

The concept and implementation of teaming has played a key role in leveraging corporate culture. Many organizations have resorted to forming workers' groups into teams. Teams now form a new way of working and learning. Some organizations even boast about the number of teams they have.

What are the attributes of teams?

- There is a trust among team members.
- There is a common purpose and vision.
- Sacrifices in individuality are demanded.
- There is discipline and guidance as to what is acceptable and what is not acceptable.
- There is team accountability.
- There is a specification of goals and associated performance indicators and measures.
- There is sharing of experience, knowledge and communication.
- There is commitment and involvement.

Working in teams and, more importantly, teaming (relationships and dynamics) have changed the configuration of corporate culture.

All the change initiatives – total quality management, customer focus, re-engineering, empowerment, teaming and other initiatives – have either leveraged or configured corporate culture. An appropriate corporate culture is one which is conducive to effective performance affecting all the drivers of business.

In some cases a change in culture has produced better performance but to sustain improved performance over the long term one has to examine other qualitative indicators of corporate culture.

Following are the considerations one needs to give in order to assess not only the quantitative but also the qualitative performance of any organization. Just because analysts have singled out certain companies as high performers financially, the true measure of performance is looking at that organization's vision and values. Vision and values should underpin all corporate activities and decisions.

Corporate vision and values

Corporate vision and corporate values are the main drivers of corporate culture. Values are standards that drive our actions and deeds and shape our behaviour. All leaders should understand the nature and the significance of values. Leaders without values become the Robert Maxwells of the corporate world.

As far back as 1992 a survey of executive opinion in the United Kingdom on 'Corporate Values – The Bottom Line Contribution' was undertaken by Digital in association with John Humble, an independent management consultant.

The authors stated ". . . the expectations and needs of managers and workers are also changing. In the UK, as elsewhere. There is a new emphasis on empowerment and accountability, and corporate structures are being adapted accordingly. In a competitive environment, people need to have the new world explained and interpreted for them, and to be coached into their new roles. Above all, they need to share the values that their company represents, and understand how they can play a part in implementing those values.

"Corporate values are the key to management of change. They are the 'glue' which binds together today's flattened, decentralized, international structures. Corporate leaders need to develop and implement values that are appropriate to the vision and strategies of the company, and ultimately to those of the company's stakeholders, including customers, employees and shareholders."

Highlights of the survey

By the term 'Corporate Values' we mean:

■ the relatively few important beliefs which are widely held to be crucial for the success of a given organization

■ those beliefs and convictions which substantially drive the behaviour of people in an organization.

How important are values?

■ 80% of organizations already have written value statements

■ 89% expect values to be more important for organizational success in the next three years, because:

     ■ "In periods of rapid change, staff need the stability and guidance of clear corporate values" (85%). And

     ■ "Properly implemented values contribute to profitability" (82%).

Top five priorities

Taking into consideration both the importance of a value and the scope for improvement in its implementation, the top priority values are:

People
"We believe our staff represent a crucial asset for our success."

Competitiveness
"We are committed to providing our customers with quality and service which beats the competitor."

Customers
"We are totally dedicated to providing our customers with service that meets their needs."

Quality
"We are committed to delivering goods and services which meet the highest objective standards."

Productivity
"We must constantly increase the productivity of every resource in the organization."

Corporate values in context

Corporate values have no meaning in isolation. They can only contribute as an integral part of the business process itself.

chapter 7

Figure 7.3 Values and
the business process.
© 1992 Digital
Equipment Company
Limited/John Humble

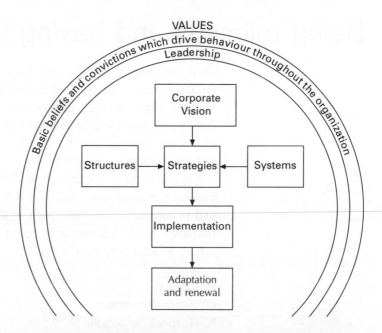

As Figure 7.3 illustrates, the starting point for the process is to set out a clear statement of "the kind of business we intend to be in the future, in the interests of our customers and staff and shareholders". This statement of Corporate Vision is a profound insight into the direction and goals of the concern.

To convert Vision into reality, top management designs Strategies ... In turn Strategies require Structures and Systems through which they can work. Implementation follows and logically a stage of learning and reflection leads to a process of Adaptation and Renewal.

Whilst that is too tidy a summary of a much richer and more complex process, in essence it is common enough in many businesses.

Where then do values fit in? The conventional wisdom is to put them in a box alongside Strategy. This is not just an error in presentation but a conceptual confusion. If the strategies and systems and so on can be crudely summarized as hardware, values are the software. Values do not fit neatly into another box. They literally permeate and influence continuously every stage of the business process.

Values in this context means those shared beliefs and convictions which really do govern people's behaviour

(Source: 'Corporate Values–The Bottom Line Contribution'. Digital Equipment Company. The survey was conducted in association with John Humble and was reported in 1992)

Being religious and having faith

Most employees conform and behave as required by their organizations. They give an outward appearance of believing their organization's mission statement and values. In any religion, what matters is not whether you go through various rituals but whether you have faith in that religion. It is the faith that is the driving force.

It is the same in organizations. Top management have to provide a mission and values and then live by them for the rest of employees to have faith in the mission and values. Recently Shell International communicated the following values to their employees:

- Integrity
- Professionalism
- Respect for people
- Pride without arrogance

These are great behavioural drivers provided they are reflected in the behaviour of the top management.

Importance of values

Values create corporate ethos. In assessing the qualitative performance of any organization one has to look at its policies in relation to employee dismissals, offering equal opportunities, avoiding organizational bullying and creating as far as possible an organizational climate free of stress.

Individual employment rights

In employment individuals have rights not to be dismissed unfairly or to be discriminated against. Various legislation lays down the minimum requirements.

There are companies who are performing very well financially. However, if you examine their records and you find that they have been reported to industrial tribunals for unfair treatment towards their employees (unfair dismissals, discrimination because of sex or colour, sexual harassment), then such companies are failing to meet their obligations towards one of their stakeholders, i.e. their employees. Such treatment and the knowledge of such treatment among existing employees will affect individual performance and subsequently organizational performance. Organizations should reinforce and enhance their performance by creating a culture of fair and just treatment towards all their employees.

Management by intimidation

In the early 1990s many companies suffered due to a severe economic recession. As a consequence massive redundancies occurred and when the economic climate started to improve many organizations streamlined their operations to follow a 'lean and mean' approach to business management.

Then came restructuring, re-engineering, de-layering and transformation which inevitably meant more loss of employment. In order to push through change programmes some managers employed intimidating tactics. "If you do not do what you are told you will join the unemployment pool." Most workers had no option but to work under such regimes. When you have commitments in terms of mortgage and family and when unemployment is very high you just grin and bear whatever is thrown at you.

Recession and competitive pressures in the 1990s have tempted some organizations to adopt harsh management practices. Some managers bully their employees to achieve the desired targets. Organizational bullying shows itself in the following ways:

- Intimidation by managers,
- Changing work practices and guidelines without any notice,
- Excessive supervision to erode self-confidence,
- Managers constantly making derisory remarks,
- Humiliating workers in front of others,
and so on.

Professor Cary Cooper of the University of Manchester Institute of Science and Technology estimates that 40 million days a year are lost each year through absenteeism caused by bullying.

Managing Performance

Cooper identifies four types of bullies:

- **Pathological bullies**: Those who simply enjoy intimidating their inferiors.
- **Situational bullies**: those who bully others when they themselves are put under pressure.
- **Role-playing bullies**: Those who emulate the authoritarian model presented by their organization.
- **Punishing bullies**: Those who love to exercise their power by punishing others.

In 1994 the BBC commissioned a survey of 1137 employees in general. The survey revealed that:

- 53 per cent believed they had been bullied at work; the victims were equally divided into men and women;
- 77% had witnessed bullying;
- in 67% of cases bullying lasted less than a year.

The concept of organizational bullying is difficult to define. At present Sweden is the only country that has a statutory definition. Bullying is defined as:

> recurrent reprehensible or distinctly negative actions which are directed against individual employees in an offensive manner and can result in those employees being placed outside the work community.

Stress at work

Stress at work is the other factor that affects individual performance. Because many organizations which have undergone transformation have fewer people than before and because these people are expected to maintain or even increase productivity, the additional workload necessitates working long hours and creates stressful situations in some circumstances.

Most senior to middle managers often work longer than official hours. According to a survey by the Institute of Management, of the 81 per cent of 1300 that took part in the survey, 55 per cent 'always' work extra hours; 54 per cent 'often or always' work at weekends.

Corporate culture – performance context

Longer hours do not necessarily enhance productivity. Working long hours also has a knock-on effect on family and personal life.

In November 1994 the High Court in the United Kingdom ruled that John Walker, a 57-year-old social worker, could sue his employers for exposing him to stress after an increase in workload resulted in a breakdown. The Health & Safety Executive estimates that more than 40 million working days a year are lost in Britain because of stress-related illnesses and that up to 60 per cent of all absences from work are caused by stress.

The main causes of stress are:

- **Occupational demands**: Demands made by particular occupations, e.g. lawyers, doctors, physicians, teachers etc. Some jobs are more stressful than others.
- **Role conflict**: Many people play different roles in their lives. Role conflict arises when an executive has different demands put upon him or her by different roles.
- **Role ambiguity**: This arises when individuals are not sure what their job is. This happens when the jobs are not properly defined or when one is not sure about the boundaries of authority and responsibility.
- **Job insecurity**: This is a common cause of stress today when organizations are constantly restructured and people made redundant.
- **Work overload and underload**: Having too much to do or not having the skills to do what is required. In the case of underload, boredom and monotony create stress.
- **Lack of competence**: Individuals are increasingly asked to face new situations which require new skills and competencies. If they do not have these skills and thus cannot meet organizational demands they suffer stress.
- **Lack of motivation**: Some individuals work for a particular organization because they have no choice. Every Monday morning they feel "Do I have to go to work today?" Such lack of inherent motivation creates stress.
- **Personal problems**: Problems at home can and do reduce performance and affect achievement. This leads to stress.

Other causes involve lack of interpersonal communication, personality clashes, bullying from superiors etc.

Managing Performance

Organizations should develop a sympathetic culture by introducing stress counselling and by monitoring stress at work as far as their employees are concerned. In the long run such measures will enhance their performance and enable organizations to retain and retrain their employees in a constantly changing climate.

Discrimination

There is now also a focus on organizations that discriminate on the grounds of age. Voluntary redundancies, enforced redundancies, and discrimination in the job market affect workers over 40 years old. In some professions such as lawyers, if you are over 30 you will find it very difficult to find a firm that will employ you.

Diversity in relation to race, religion, colour, gender, age, disability and so on is the source of creativity in an organization. Some organizations that proclaim an equal opportunities culture do not really implement such a policy in practice. Such organizations need to communicate their equal opportunities policy effectively to all managers and employees, and only objective job-related criteria should be used to recruit and promote workers. Such criteria will bring about high performance.

The Institute of Personnel and Development in the UK is committed to the removal of age discrimination in employment because it considers such practice wasteful of talent; it creates inappropriate use of knowledge and experience and age is a poor predictor of performance.

A culture devoted to fair and just treatment, tolerance of all employees, diversity, sympathy, creativity, learning, empowerment and delivering service excellence will make organizations responsive to the marketplace.

TIME OUT

Examine aspects of the qualitative performance of your organization.

1. How many unfair dismissal cases has your company had over the past year?

_____

2. What is the rate of absenteeism per year?

_____

3. Are there any cases of discrimination or alleged discrimination?

_____

4. Are there any cases or alleged cases of organizational bullying or sexual harassment?
5. In your opinion, what kind of culture does your organization have? Tick the appropriate culture:

   a. Culture of service
   b. Culture of respect
   c. Culture of trust
   d. Culture of profit first
   e. Culture of open communication
   f. Culture of business results
   g. Culture of minimum communication
   h. Culture of collaboration (internally)
   i. Culture of 'dog eat dog'
   j. Culture of recognition of employees

6. In a few words indicate 'the way we do business in our organization'.

_____

_____

_____

7. Do you know what values and beliefs your organization has?
8. Are values and beliefs communicated successfully throughout your organization?
9. In recruiting staff do you have an induction programme to make new recruits conversant with your organization's culture?
10. Some top management believe culture is a 'soft' thing. "Real leaders do not talk about culture." What is your own view regarding the importance of organizational culture and its impact on individual and organizational performance?

Modern organizations are conglomerates of diversity – diversity of personalities, skills, gender, race, nationalities, values, behaviours and so on. How diversities are managed and balanced affects corporate performance.

Managing diversity for corporate performance

The following statement captures the essence of the meaning and the importance of managing diversity:

What is 'managing diversity'?

Managing diversity is about consciously adding into the equal opportunities mix such ingredients as age, personality, personal and corporate background, lifestyle, values and even sexual preferences in a way that delivers improved corporate performance.

Employees are whole people, each very different from the next in myriad ways; managing diversity explicitly recognizes this and seeks to create an environment in which the full potential of all employees can be tapped in the pursuit of corporate objectives.

(Source: 'Managing Diversity and the new Deal' by Jane O'Sullivan, consultant at Towers Perrin. *Perspectives*, November 1996)

In the same article Jane O'Sullivan goes on to present the following perspectives on the changing needs of employers and employees and the emergence of the new employment deal:

Old deal	**Perceived deal today**	**New deal**
If You:	**If You:**	**If you:**
Are loyal	Develop skills we need	Develop skills we need
Work hard	Apply them in ways that	Apply them in ways that help
Fulfil obligations	help the company	the company succeed
	succeed	Behave consistently with our
	Behave consistently with	new values
	our new values	

We'll provide:		**We'll provide:**
A secure job		A challenging work
Steady pay increases	**We'll provide:**	environment
Financial security	A job if we can	Support for your development
	Gestures that we care	Reward for your contribution
	The same pay	

And you'll be part of:	**And you'll be part of**	**And you'll be part of:**
A secure industry	A business in **crisis**	A revitalized industry leader

How long does it take to change organizational culture?

The speed of change depends on the size and the nature of the organization. What is important, however, is knowing why you want to change and how you are going to do it. My experience has been to adopt 'shock therapy'. What is happening in practice, however, is that many organizations depend on change consultants and organization development experts to do analysis and change their organizations. Consultants, for their own benefit, spend too much time on 'psychoanalysing' the organization and do not get down to the nitty gritty of changing behaviour. People in organizations should bring about changes themselves and the role of consultants should be 'hand-holding' in the initial stages.

British Airways adopted 'shock therapy' when changing from a public corporation to a privatized company. Over the years the company has been involved in fine-tuning its culture in order to respond to the marketplace. Some of the initiatives undertaken by companies like British Airways, Federal Express, Motorola, Sun Microsystems and so on bring about change in organizational culture without singling out or focusing on corporate culture.

For example, at Sun Microsystems they have introduced an Employee Quality Index in order to improve their employees' work effectiveness and satisfaction. The instrument is designed to drive out 'performance inhibitors' – the things that prevent someone from performing at their best or make work tasks more difficult to accomplish.

Eliminating or minimizing 'performance inhibitors' is bound to change 'the way we do things here'. In other words, the by-product of the Employee Quality Index is a corporate culture audit and a change in corporate culture. If you consider other initiatives undertaken by Sun Microsystems, such as the Customer Satisfaction and Customer Loyalty Indices, they will all impact on corporate culture and yet nowhere in their communications to employees is corporate culture mentioned.

Managing the qualitative performance of any organization must involve examining the corporate culture which incorporates the values, beliefs and behaviour of the total organization. Corporate culture should be one of the key components of managing balanced performance.

Selected reading

Drennan, D. (1992). *Transforming Company Culture*. McGraw-Hill.

Kermally, S. (1996). *Total Management Thinking*. Butterworth-Heinemann.

The Economist Intelligence Unit (1993). Managing Cultural Differences for Competitive Advantage.

Spencer, J. and Pruss, A. (19). *How To Implement Change in Your Company*. Piatkus.

Morin, W. J. (1995). Mending the Crisis in Corporate Values. *Management Review*, July.

8

Economic performance

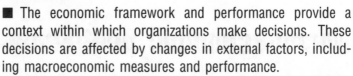

in brief

The key to an economic way of thinking lies not in the way economists think, but in the things they think about.

Unknown

Summary

■ The economic framework and performance provide a context within which organizations make decisions. These decisions are affected by changes in external factors, including macroeconomic measures and performance.

■ Understanding the macroeconomic framework helps organizations to sharpen their decision making and corporate strategy.

■ The macroeconomic framework relates to investment, savings, foreign exchange fluctuations, inflation, employment and economic growth.

■ The competitiveness of the nation incorporates high performance of all organizations.

■ Economic and Monetary Union and the Single Currency will affect the competitiveness of all organizations.

■ Organizations have to take action NOW in order to be global players and prepare themselves for the year 2000.

■ How to do so will depend on the extent to which they follow three key guidelines: (1) paying attention to six Es of performance management, (2) keeping score of achievements and performance and (3) focusing on customer retention and loyalty.

Managing Performance

If organizations manage their performance effectively the result will be:

- They will be able to track their strategy effectively.
- They will be able to compete successfully.
- They will make a contribution to the economic well-being of their country.
- In turn customers have more spending power.

The richer the nation becomes, the more organizations benefit in trading their goods and services.

In economics, a distinction is made between micro-economics and macroeconomics. Micro-economics focuses on business organizations whereas macroeconomics deals with the workings of the whole economy.

The economic system within which organizations operate concerns itself with three fundamental questions: (a) how the economy produces goods and services, (b) what is being produced and (c) for whom goods and services are being produced. Price determines how and where resources are allocated and the markets bring together customers, consumers and suppliers of goods and services.

Micro-economic performance

In focusing its attention on individual enterprises, micro-economics deals with prices, costs and markets. In reality there is much more to business operations and decisions than these. In order to remain competitive in national and global markets, organizations nowadays have to pay special attention to the three Ps of business: people, processes and products.

People

Organizations have to pay special attention to their employees in order to compete effectively. Paying attention to their employees means recruiting and selecting people who are willing to perform specific functions but at the same time willing to be trained in different skills; they have to work in multi-functional teams; they have to be prepared to make decisions and assume the responsibility to do so.

Organizations have to institute performance systems to monitor their employees' performance and their competencies. Emphasis has to be put on enhancing and measuring employees' performance.

Also, in these days of globalization, organizations are employing not only multi-skilled but multi-cultural workforces. Managing such a workforce has been one of the major challenges facing organizations. This challenge will be accentuated in the new millennium as the world becomes technologically closer.

Processes

In the 1990s organizations switched their attention to processes in order to be responsive to market needs. Processes were re-engineered and organizations' structures flattened to enable organizations to get close to their customers. For example, AT&T Global Business reduced order processing tenfold and achieved a 35 per cent reduction in headcount. Texas Instruments reduced process cycle time by well over 50 per cent.

There are numerous examples of organizations in America, Europe and Asia-Pacific going through re-engineering processes to become slim and fast.

Products

Because of intensive competition, product life cycles are becoming dramatically short. Organizations have to be at the cutting edge of product innovation. For example, Kodak re-engineered its product development process by introducing concurrent engineering. It introduced its new disposable camera in 35 rather than 70 weeks. Hall Mark reduced their new product development cycle from between two and three years to one. IBM embarked upon a project to examine all the operational processes that take products from the drawing board to the customers.

Managing Performance

The three Ps of organizations (people, processes and products) have an impact on the markets, revenue and costs which constitute the subject of micro-economics.

The quality of people, processes and products became the battlecry in the 1980s under the umbrella of total quality management. The cornerstone of total quality management is customer satisfaction.

Total quality management is concerned with continuous improvement in performance in satisfying customer needs. In 1987 the Baldrige National Quality Award was instituted in the USA and in 1992 the European Quality Award was launched in Europe. The objectives of both awards were to enable organizations constantly to monitor and improve their performance in relation to their people, processes and products.

All the chapters in this book have been geared to looking at performance management at the micro or organizational level. Managing performance successfully affects the performance of the nation's economy as a whole (the macroeconomics level). In turn, micro-economic variables affect business decisions and business performance.

What is macroeconomics?

Unfortunately very few managers are interested in understanding the workings of the macroeconomic system. The economic environment impacts business decisions and corporate strategies should be formulated within the context of the existing and future performance of macroeconomic variables.

To understand the nature of the global economy it is important first to understand the economic framework and structure of a nation. The best way to get a panoramic view of the economic system is to look at it in terms of the circular flow of income and goods and services. See Figure 8.1.

Imagine an economy made up of customers and organizations producing goods and services. Customers spend all their earnings as soon as they receive them and organizations sell all their products and services as soon as they produce them. The circular flow of income and expenditure will look as shown in Figure 8.1.

Economic performance

Figure 8.1 Economic system

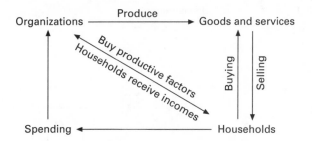

The total of all customers' earnings (wages, interest, rent, profit received) is called income. The total income received is called the **national income**. The total monetary value of all goods and services supplied in the economy is called the **national product**.

In the real world, however, customers do not instantly spend all their income on goods and services. They may and do save part of their income. The difference between their income and their expenditure is called **savings**. Secondly, organizations do not instantly sell all the goods and services they produce. When organizations accumulate a stock of finished products or raw materials, in economic terms they are said to engage in **inventory investment**. When they buy machinery or new technology or build plant and factories they are said to engage in **fixed investment**. In Figure 8.1, what customers do not spend constitutes savings and what organizations do not sell constitutes investments.

Income minus expenditure = savings
Production minus sales = investment
Income = production
Therefore, savings = investments

To maintain the stability of the economic system, savings in an economy should be equal to investments. To promote economic growth and improve the economic performance of a nation, organizations, in the face of severe competition, have to generate more income so that their customers can spend more. To do so they have to focus their attention on continuously improving their products, processes and people.

However, again in the real world, it is difficult to achieve a neat equilibrium between savings and investments. Savings sometimes exceed investment and in some situations investments exceed savings. This is where the skill of managing the economy comes into play.

Managing Performance

Figure 8.2 Flow of savings and investments

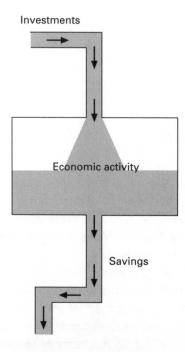

If we take the analogy of a water tank and water system (Figure 8.2), the level of water in a tank is the level of economic activity in a nation. The outflow is savings and the inflow of water is investments. When outflow exceeds inflow the level of water will fall. When savings exceed investment the level of economic activity falls and there is **unemployment** in the economy. When the inflow of water exceeds outflow the level of water will rise. When investments exceed savings the level of economic activity will rise and there is a possibility of **inflation** if the economy is not managed properly. The economic performance of a nation is related to the fluctuations in savings and investments. These in turn depend on the behaviour of customers and organizations.

To control fluctuations in savings and investments and at the same time improve economic performance, governments have at their disposal various instruments which are categorized as monetary instruments (increase or decrease in money supply, changes in interest rates) and fiscal instruments (changes in taxation, allowances and grants). Employment of the instruments affects organizations and customers.

The changes in the national economy have repercussions on international transactions. For example, let us assume that country 'A' has a very high level of economic activity as a consequence of investments exceeding savings. The high level of customers' expenditure will create demand for goods and services which in turn will create demand for resources. The prices of these will increase if demand is in excess of supply and as a result the prices of goods and services will increase. High prices will mean that country 'A' will become expensive and goods from other countries (imports) will become relatively cheaper. Country 'A's exports will fall and imports will increase, thus creating an unfavourable trade balance.

As a result of a weak trade balance, speculators will get rid of country 'A's currencies and buy and hold the currencies of other countries with a strong economy. This action on the part of speculators will accentuate country 'A's economic problem. The government of country 'A' will be prompted to take appropriate economic measures which will affect the decision making of customers and organizations.

The excess of savings over investments will result in a falling level of economic activity and there will be unemployment and the prices of goods and services will fall. Again, appropriate measures taken by the government will impact on the decision making of customers and organizations. Figure 8.3 demonstrates the effects of different economic scenarios.

Exports in excess of imports

Favourable trade

Strong currency. Speculators will demand this currency

Price of currency of country 'A' will increase in foreign exchange market

Country 'A's exports will become expensive

Country 'A's exports will fall. Imports to country 'A' will increase

Country 'A' will have unfavourable trade balance

Measures will be undertaken to rectify the situation.
These measures will affect organizations and customers

Figure 8.3 Economic scenarios from a favourable to an unfavourable trade position of country 'A'

Managing Performance

When organizations are put under pressure to perform better than their competitors they try to improve the productivity of the resources they use to supply goods and services. At the national level, growth, productivity and employment constitute key indicators of competitiveness.

To be competitive means to satisfy customers wherever they may be. In countries like the USA, Sweden and Germany there are customer satisfaction indices which show the level of customer satisfaction. According to Professor Claes Fornell, founder of both the Swedish Customer Satisfaction Barometer and the American Customer Satisfaction Index, it is imperative for countries to monitor quality performance from the customers' perspective. He says that traditional measures of macroeconomic performance provide an incomplete picture of economic performance and a nation's competitiveness. What drives economic performance is quality and high customer satisfaction. The customer satisfaction index should be an important macroeconomic indicator in its own right.

Managing performance globally

The world of competitiveness is changing very quickly. A few decades ago it was divided into developed countries (USA, Western Europe) and under-developed countries (mainly Asian and African countries). Three decades later we read about 'Asian Tigers' competing fiercely with so-called developed nations.

Singapore is ahead of all other nations and they are increasing their lead. Japan, which dominated the competitiveness table so strongly in the past, is currently fourth in the table. The European countries are more dispersed, thus underlining the difficulty they are experiencing in their efforts to converge their economies, a prerequisite of the Maastricht Treaty.

The dynamism of east Asia remains staggering. Next to Singapore, Hong Kong is showing strong performance. Taiwan also produced a formidable performance in 1996.

In 1995 Coopers & Lybrand undertook a survey soliciting the views of European business leaders on business competitiveness. The survey analysed nearly 1000 business leaders in four EU countries – Germany, France, Italy and the United Kingdom.

Key messages of survey findings

■ Recession affected turnover of one third of sample companies. Revenue fell between 1990 and 1995. German companies, particularly exporters, performed considerably worse than companies in the other three countries. In contrast, the greater number of higher turnover growth companies was in the UK.

■ Over half of all companies in France, Germany and the UK have reduced the number of their employees in the last five years.

■ The level of competition facing European business, as distinct from the ability of companies to compete successfully, is perceived to be strong and has increased significantly over the last five years.

■ The overall increase in the degree of competition experienced by European business is further accentuated by the global growth of competition from traditional economies, primarily the EU and North America and, increasingly, from the emerging economies in China, South East Asia and Eastern Europe. German companies show a much stronger focus on 'near' countries as competitive threats, particularly in eastern Europe; France, Italy and the UK focus on the 'far' sources of competition, especially North America, China, Japan and South East Asia.

■ Many European businesses believe they can meet the challenge posed by low prices from east European and far Eastern competitors through non-price factors such as industry experience and leading-edge products.

■ Many businesses, and manufacturing and construction companies in particular, have sought to improve their competitiveness by taking actions to reduce costs and increase productivity.

■ In addition to cost reduction, European businesses, particularly in manufacturing and construction, have responded to increased competition by becoming more innovative.

■ The competitive standing of companies depends, however, not only on their own actions but also on the factors influencing the external environment which may help or hinder their competitive positions. The availability of highly qualified labour is believed to have helped European business to compete more than any other external factor. Other 'helping' factors are economic conditions and the availability of capital.

Managing Performance

■ In terms of 'hindering' factors, national economic conditions are perceived to be the most important hindrance for Italian companies and the second most important for France and the UK.

■ In relation to European Monetary Union and the Single Currency, business leaders in all four of Europe's leading economies are strongly in favour of moving towards EMU and the Single Currency as soon as economic conditions permit. Not only will this reduce costs by reducing exchange rate risks, business leaders believe it will also contribute to greater economic stability in Europe and thus help their competitiveness.

■ Looking ahead, it is to be expected that global trade flows will increase. The pattern of these flows will change significantly as countries learn how to exploit more effectively their comparative advantages. European businesses need to plan how to take advantage of these trends.

(Source: Executive Briefing: Competitiveness – Focus on success. Coopers & Lybrand, 1995)

EMU, competitiveness and organizational performance

Several years ago, the Maastricht treaty committed the European Union to the goal of economic and monetary union (EMU). According to the European Commission, the transition to EMU will have important beneficial effects on competitiveness as regards both internal and external aspects.

Internally, EMU will eliminate transaction costs of cross border payments. In addition, it will foster competitiveness through increasing transparency. SMEs whose costs in participating in international trade are at present relatively high, will particularly benefit, as EMU will enable them to increase their efficiency by entering into all European markets.

Furthermore, EMU will contribute significantly to exploit the full advantages of the internal market. The past four years have witnessed that currency fluctuations have led to a suboptimal allocation of production factors, jeopardizing the beneficial effect of economic integration and slowing down growth in Europe.

Externally, given the importance of the European Union in international trade, financial markets may grant to the Euro a status of international currency, similar to that enjoyed by the Dollar. European companies will progressively be able to sell in Euro on third markets and will thus be safeguarded from the effects of currency changes on sale prices.

Finally, macroeconomic policies play a central role for competitiveness. In particular, public deficits which are too high absorb a considerable share of private savings (nearly 35% in 1993) to the detriment of productive investments and push interest rates higher. Policies oriented towards budgetary stability allow the macroeconomic framework to be improved. Indeed, general government net borrowing decreased from 6.3% in 1993 in the EU to 5.1% in 1995 and 4.4% in 1996 (forecasts). Real short-term interest rates have followed a similar path, falling from 6.7% in 1992 to 4.9% in 1993 and 3.9% in 1995. This development is reinforced by progress towards Economic and Monetary Union.

(Source: Paper on 'Benchmarking The Competitiveness of European Industry' presented by the European Commission to the Conference with the Government of Italy organized by Business International and the Economist Conferences, Autumn 1996.)

The Coopers and Lybrand survey indicated that business leaders in Germany, France, Italy and the United Kingdom are strongly in favour of moving towards EMU and the Single Currency.

In the report published by the Economist Intelligence Unit on 'Pros and Cons of EMU', the downside of EMU is envisaged in a 'Europeanizing' of labour markets across the EMU area. There is a possibility of harmonizing regulation of Europe's labour markets through the EU's Social Chapter.

The report also states that the Euro could itself prove a volatile, if not a weak, currency, because of market uncertainties over the policies adopted by the European Central Bank.

The report concludes: "We do expect EMU to happen. Far more tentatively, we expect it to be a partial success though not necessarily for all its members . . ."

TIME OUT

Managing Performance

What effect will EMU have on your business and why?

_____

_____

_____

_____

_____

What are the implications for managing performance?

1. Organizations constantly have to monitor their strategy and measure their performance.
2. To compete successfully they have to enhance their non-price factors to face competition from eastern European and far Eastern countries.
3. Non-price factors mean sustaining total quality improvement within and throughout the organizations; reviewing competencies to continuously improve organizational capability; being innovative in product development; eliminating non-value-adding activities and processes; maintaining and even increasing investment in training and research and development.
4. The primary responsibility for ensuring that organizations remain competitive lies with organizations themselves. According to the European Commission, organizations maintain competitiveness through the efficiency and flexibility with which they satisfy existing market needs and through their ability to adjust to structural change, to create new markets and to meet new needs.

Preparing for the new millennium – Welcome year 2000

A Focus on six 'E's of managing performance

1. Economy: The cost of all the inputs of an organization. Organizations should analyse all the inputs and acquire them at least monetary cost. This is what sourcing globally is all about. Because of globalization and developments in telecommunication and computer technology, access to global networks becomes possible and facilitates global sourcing.

2. Efficiency. Efficiency refers to the relationship between input and output and it is usually expressed as a ratio. Having obtained low-cost inputs they should be utilized and deployed productively. The focus should be on productivity – producing more with same inputs or producing more with proportionally fewer inputs.

3. Effectiveness. Achieving the objectives an organization set out to achieve. Objectives need to be constantly reviewed and revised because of changes in external factors. Organizations need a flexible structure and capable workforce to deliver what they set out to achieve.

4. Environment. Environmental considerations are acquiring more attention from various stakeholders. It was reported (*Financial Times*, 24 February 1997) that a group of shareholders was to press Shell at its annual meeting in May, 1997 to publish regular audits of the oil group's social and environmental performance.

    We have seen in Nissan's case study that considering environmental factors meant enhancing the efficiency of Nissan's financial and operational performance. According to Professor Michael Porter, 'guru' of corporate strategy, environmental considerations 'force' organizations to be creative.

5. Employees. As far as employees are concerned, organizations should invest in their employees to enable them to gain new competencies. Organizational capabilities depend on the competencies of the organization's employees.

6. Ethics. Leaders not only must lead but they also must follow. How they lead and follow depends on their own personal values and the values they want to impress upon the organizations they lead. Their values and their mission will drive the performance of their organizations.

B Keep score of achievements and performance

Organizations need maps of their journey and destination and they constantly have to review their routes and keep score of their achievements. Scorecards should incorporate various perspectives that drive performance.

Professor Kaplan has given us the basic framework. The responsibility falls on all organizations to adopt and adapt scorecards according to their needs and the nature of their business.

C Differentiate on the basis of your customers and employees

Organizations should not shift their focus from customers. It is very easy and tempting to get involved in measuring everything and get into the 'measurement trap', thereby forgetting the *raison d'être* of organizations. The differentiating factor in the new millennium is going to be focusing on customers' needs, retention and loyalty. Yes, many organizations in the 1990s have attempted to be customer-driven, but paying lip service, as some organizations have done, is not enough. The true measure of survival and performance is going to be customer retention and loyalty. And it is important to bear in mind that it is not systems but people who deliver customer service.

Selected reading

The Economist Intelligence Unit (1997). Pros and cons of EMU.
Coopers and Lybrand (1995). *The Coopers and Lybrand Competitive Survey*, 1995.
Begg, D. (4th edn, 1994). *Economics*. McGraw-Hill.
Johnson, M. (1996). *The Aspiring Manager's Survival Guide*. Butterworth-Heinemann.

Conclusion: A to Z of managing performance

A: Align corporate mission and objectives with departmental/team and individual objectives.

B: Business performance should incorporate the interests of all stakeholders.

C: Clarify your intention and communicate clearly and with conviction.

D: Develop measures which are consistent with business objectives.

E: Evaluate performance regularly.

F: Feedback system should be appropriate and should be considered seriously.

Focus on internal and external factors that drive your business.

G: Generate enthusiasm and commitment through your leadership.

H: Have courage of your convictions.

I: Improvement should be continuous. Invest in your products, processes and people.

J: Juggle with various business drivers to design a balanced performance system.

K: Keep scorecards to track performance.

L: Learning and innovation are key drivers of enhanced performance.

M: Mission statement should be made meaningful to all employees and it should be a motivating statement.

Managing Performance

N: Non-financial measures are just as important in measurement as financial measures.

O: Openness in communication will lead to outperforming your targets.

P: People, processes and products should be monitored continuously to achieve high performance.

Q: Quality should be a primary consideration in all activities and operations.

R: Review for desired results regularly.

S: Set stretching targets for enhanced performance.

T: Teaming and teambuilding should be aligned to divisional and individual objectives.

U: Understand what your measurement system is all about.

V: Vision of your organization should be the centrepiece of the measurement system. Values should underpin the measurement system.

W: Wow! factor in the business world results from managing performance effectively.

X: Theory X approach which takes a pessimistic view of motivation should be made redundant in designing the performance system.

Y: Your success depends on your conviction, commitment and communication.

Z: Zeal, zest and zing of all employees need to be sustained by enlightened leadership.

Index

Index

Index